Sincerely Yours
A. Schuyler

THE INCARNATE WORD,

AND OTHER SERMONS

BY

ANTHONY SCHUYLER, D. D.

Rector of Grace Church, Orange, N. J.

NEW YORK
THOMAS WHITTAKER
2 AND 3 BIBLE HOUSE
1898

Wipf and Stock Publishers
199 W 8th Ave, Suite 3
Eugene, OR 97401

The Incarnate Word, and Other Sermons
By Schuyler, Anthony
Softcover ISBN-13: 978-1-7252-9116-4
Hardcover ISBN-13: 978-1-7252-9115-7
eBook ISBN-13: 978-1-7252-9117-1
Publication date 11/2/2020
Previously published by Thomas Whittaker, 1898

This edition is a scanned facsimile of
the original edition published in 1898.

PREFATORY NOTE

THESE sermons were preached in Grace Church, Orange, New Jersey, in the course of a pastorate of thirty years. The publication of a selection of plain unconnected parochial sermons, scattered through a series of years, originated in no thought of the author. He yields to the judgment of those who, having heard the sermons preached, think the reading of them will prove useful to themselves and others.

A. S.

CONTENTS

CHAPTER	PAGE
I. The Incarnate Word	7
II. The Year of the Church—Sermon for Advent	18
III. Christ's Coming in Infancy—Christmas	29
IV. The Tree of Life	39
V. Popular Prejudices Against the Gospels	52
VI. The Prayer of the Syro-Phenician Woman	66
VII. Fasting for Christ's Sake	78
VIII. How to do the Will of God	87
IX. Limits of the Divine Patience	100
X. Peace in Believing	111
XI. The Sin of the Prodigal Son	122
XII. The Test of Christian Discipleship	134
XIII. Enmity through Sin and Reconciliation through Christ—For Good Friday	145
XIV. Incredible Alternatives to the Resurrection of the Dead—For Easter Day	157
XV. Grieving the Spirit—For Whitsunday	167
XVI. The Threefold Name—For Trinity Sunday	176
XVII. Christianity an Embodied and Unchangeable Religion	189
XVIII. Faith Triumphing over Disappointments	201
XIX. Coming to Jesus by Night	212
XX. The Conversion of Zaccheus or the Power of Sympathy	224
XXI. Sermon for All Saints' Day	237

I.

THE INCARNATE WORD.

"The Seed is the Word of God."—St. Luke viii. 11.

THE phrase "The Word of God," is largely used throughout the Scriptures. The first two verses of the Gospel according to St. John seem to suggest its meaning as well in other places as there, to be the person of our Lord Jesus Christ. There He is declared to be both the Word and God, and so the Word of God. It is a remarkable and suggestive appellation considering the frequency of its use in the Scriptures.

Of the opening verses of the Fourth Gospel, a noted scholar and preacher in the English Church [1] has said—"I do not pretend to be able to explain this text. No man can comprehend it but He of whom it speaks, Jesus Christ, the Word of God." In the text we have it that "the seed is the Word of God." We call Holy Scripture the Word of God. It is the oldest and the commonest designation of

[1] Kingsley's Village Sermons, p. 256.

the sacred writings, and it came from adopting for its name the phrase as it stands in the Scripture. What is fairly to be inferred from this, is that the Word of God is not to be restricted to that which is written in the Scriptures. It stands in St. John's Gospel and it stands here, in our Lord's explanation of the parable of the Sower, as though there were indeed but one grand Utterance and one central seminal "Word of God" upon which all other words of His depend, or out of which they grow for the meaning we are to give them.

If this be the case, we have the key to that meaning in the person of Jesus Christ Himself, to wit:—that He is both the Sower and the Seed; that is, He sows Himself throughout the written Word, the Scriptures. A late writer in view of the comparative lack of significance in the word "Bible," and impressed with the importance of giving true names to things, suggests this title to the Book, namely—"A History of Human Redemption and of God's Dealings with Men to this End." Such a title would, no doubt, facilitate the investigation of the scholar, and render needless much of the criticism, literary and otherwise, that has gone on with the Scriptures as a wide and unenclosed field, and tending to shake our old time reverence for and faith in them. If the Bible is a mere book or series of books, its language must, of course, be interpreted like that of other books. As such it is mingled history, prophecy, poetry, allegory and so on, and must be interpreted according to rules that bring out of other books their meaning. But if Christ in person, and in His mission to the world, is the one grand utterance of God's will to man, to which all others are subordinate, then there are two sides to the Holy Scriptures as the Word of God. And it depends upon our attention to both, but especially to the side where their key is, whether we shall be able to retain our faith in them, in the face of the criticism that is going on.

One side is, of course, the human side, and that is just as surely in Scripture as the Divine is in it. Reading it we are reading the words of men and the thoughts of men, their reasonings, their feelings and their experiences. And they must needs be so regarded. The writers moved about among men, undistinguished outwardly from men among whom they moved, with all the human limitations of their fellows, but charged and burdened nevertheless, consciously or unconsciously, with an unearthly message to their fellow men,—just as our Lord and Saviour Himself moved among men as truly a man as any of them, and yet with a heavenly mission. And here, possibly is one great difficulty that men nowadays find with the Bible. They take the letter and the apparent drift here and there, as though there were nothing under it and nothing higher in it than human learning can discover, from the books of writers like themselves.

And following out the same idea, they might say, as some do, that the Saviour Himself was a man, however wise and good, and nothing beyond it. Is this the true standpoint of Scripture investigation and interpretation? Supposing it all true, that they take for granted, or discover for themselves in the Scriptures—is this the only side of that which we call the Bible or Word of God? If so, it is a delusive designation. It means nothing vital to the interests of human beings, and the Book might be freely handled by critics or put away from this time forth. We should lose something of ancient history, and something of sound moral teaching. But considering that there are books unmixed with hard things and humanly credible, that may be read and pondered to something of the same moral effect, with less of labor or learning, why should these fragments of man's device be pored over to the puzzling of men's minds?

No, my dear Brethren: there is another side

to the Holy Scriptures. There is something which enables us to bring these fragments together and make them one, from the Book of Genesis to that of Revelation. There is a golden thread of unity that pervades and ties them all together. Fragmentary writings they may be called and so we call some historical, and some unhistorical, or legendary, and others mythical and allegorical books. Even so they may be. Nevertheless, like the different parts of the human body, they are fragments, each and every one of which has its place. An overruling power breathes for those who will believe it, the breath of life into them. The careful, serious reader of Scripture who will read in the peradventure that this is the truth, will find it to be even so.

To the question what is this one Word of God that binds together in a harmonious whole the history, prophecy, allegory and poetry of so many men, through so many generations of the race, from Genesis to Revelation, there is but one answer, and it is the only solution of that which must otherwise remain a puzzle or a series of puzzles harder to believe than any miracle recorded in the Old Testament or the New. The solution is that Jesus Christ, born late in time into this world, as the seed of a woman, was from the foundation of the world and is the one emphatic and all pervading Word of God to man.

It has been said by a free pulpit handler of Scripture, that credulity will find Christ in every book of the Old Testament as well as the New,—find Him in the first chapter of Genesis, —find His Gospel in the prophecy of Ezekiel, and find Him in almost every psalm of David. But what except credulity can believe the Bible to contain the Word of God in any tolerable sense of that expression, and yet sees Christ only in the New Testament and confines Him there to His life on earth of three and thirty years however, He may be called and deemed a consummate man and the flower of our humanity. All of us are ready to call Him this. But many deny to Him His claim to be the Seed as well as the flower and the fruit. They deny that He was the one Word proceeding out of the mouth of God to man that gives meaning, cohesion and character to what holy men have written. I know it is said, in order to believe this, that we must believe Christ Himself to be a miracle harder to be believed than the strangest and most incredible statement of the Sacred Record. For was He not a man like ourselves? Did He not come into the world as we do? Did He not depend, as we do, in His childhood and youth upon the ceaseless ministry of parents and others? And did not His kinsfolk and acquaintance all know it, and did they not speak the truth about Him when they asked "Is not this the carpenter?"— and "His brothers and sisters, are they not here with us?" And did He not hunger and thirst and suffer and die and go the way of all the earth?

Yes. All this is true of Him and precious as true. It was true to the eye of sense then, and it is true to the eyes that read it and the ears that hear it now. Only the Book we call the Bible, or the Word of God, is inexplicable and undeserving Christian attention on the supposition that Christ was nothing more or higher than He thus appeared to be. We must give up the Book as the Word of God, or take Christ to be far other and higher than this. Suppose then, that this same Jesus was and is the one grand utterance of the Word and wisdom of Almighty God to man throughout the ages, and what then? What indeed, but that Scripture must be interpreted in accordance with this pervading truth.

And why should it be a strange or incredible truth to beings, who under all that they appear to men to be, yet have invisible and immortal souls? This is the only assumption upon which you can explain the enigma of a human being, or believe him to be different, in any important sense, from the brutes that perish. If God has given to man a higher nature that we cannot see, why should He not have brought to light in some way (and is there any other way than He has taken in the Scripture) the promise and the pledge, the seed and the beginning of that which is higher still in Jesus Christ, and that is the divine in the human, God with us. Thus was "the Word made flesh and dwelt among us." He appeared as flesh in the Sacred Story, and ceased not so to appear till the record closes and dismisses Him to the Heavens from whence He came, and takes final leave of Him, not without tokens and assurances of His coming again in power and great glory, at the end of the present frame of things.

My brethren—I have given you here, I solemnly believe, the key to the unlocking of all the really concerning truths to us, of the Old and the New Testament. I have given you that which only can secure your faith in and reverence for the revelation therein of God's will to man, there to remain unaffected by any advancement in mere human learning present or to come. All I have said is already summed up for us, so far as the Old Testament is concerned, in the words of Christ Himself [1]— "Ye

[1] St. John v. 39. Rev. Version.

search the Scriptures, for in them ye think ye have eternal life. And these are they that bear witness of me, and ye will not come to me that ye may have life."

Let me go on to say that here as elsewhere, in matters of far less consequence, there are now as there have ever been, and it is feared, ever will be, two classes or sorts of mind. The one class takes what first strikes and engages its attention to be the whole truth with which it has to do. Mastering that, it forthwith dismisses the subject as once for all exhausted. The other class looks farther, according as its curiosity, or, what is of more importance, its own felt needs, suggest. So it was in the days of the Saviour's flesh. One set of people quickly made up its mind from what it knew. Oh yes, we know this man from whence He is. We know His origin. We know His condition in life. We knew His father and mother and His occupation. We hear indeed something more. There is a rumor. There is the appearance of uncommon wisdom in Him and of miraculous gifts. But knowing already who and what He was and is, we pronounce the rumor false, and that a delusion has seized hold of people about Him. And so they dismissed Him from their thoughts as having no further concern with an already familiar subject.

On the other hand were the twelve disciples mingling among these doubters and deniers. They also knew what others knew, and yet they had come to believe a great deal more. They pondered His words together with His works and found in them something of their mighty meaning. And while they were doing this He stood before them, giving back to them the unspoken thoughts of their own hearts, till to them He grew to be more than any man,— even the one great utterance, or Word of God, —having the words of eternal life upon His lips, and embodying in Himself the light and love and power of heaven on this earth. And they said—" Is not this He that should come? —Is not this He of whom Moses in the law and the prophets did write?" And they said— " Rabbi, thou art the Son of God: Thou are the King of Israel." They were drawn on even beyond this, until the most skeptical among them voiced the faith of all in the words— " My Lord and my God!"

Need I say that we witness to-day the same division because of Him? So that the work of the Church in this day of light and knowledge and broader and deeper human learning, is just that of His apostles over again, in the first age of Christianity. And that work is to rebind the broken and written word of God into one continuous revelation of the Word made flesh lest He, the very Seed of life, be lost or caught away out of the record that holy men moved by the Holy Ghost have made.

When this is gone then all is gone out of the word of God that has the power to regenerate and save the world.

One word in conclusion, and that is a solemn admonition to you who are before me. Cherish the written word but only as you would cherish the casket of a priceless jewel there enshrined, and a jewel that would otherwise be lost to yourselves and will surely be lost to a world that will never know its preciousness. In all your readings and searchings and ponderings of Scripture, never forget or make second the finding and appropriation to yourselves of the one hid treasure in that field. Find, in other words, the golden thread that runs through the warp and woof of man's device in the Sacred Volume. Be sure, either through or under its many words, some strange, others to your mind contradictory, and many hard to be understood, that you have laid hold in Jesus Christ of the one emphatic Word of God, the key to all that really concerns you here, or hereafter. And let that Word be in you as seed springing up and bringing forth fruit to everlasting life.

II.

THE YEAR OF THE CHURCH—SERMON FOR ADVENT.

"It seemed good to me also, having had perfect understanding of all these things from the very first, to write unto thee in order, most excellent Theophilus."

"That thou mightest know the certainty of those things wherein thou hast been instructed."—St. Luke i. 3, 4.

THE knowing religious truth with certainty is declared here to be the result of setting forth the things to be known in their order.—And the things referred to are the things concerning Christ; His earthly history from its supernatural beginning, to His final Ascension into heaven. With this the Gospel of St. Luke closes.

Then follows the second treatise of this Evangelist the "Acts of the Apostles." It takes up the narrative at the point where his Gospel closes, and carries it orderly on through the period of the founding and extension of the Church. It begins with a reference to the former treatise of which he speaks as a treatise "of all that Jesus began to do and to teach."

The gospel of St. Luke is not only fuller at the beginning and the close of Christ's earthly life than the others, but it is more consecutive as regards time and event. All this as St. Luke declares in the text, "that we may know the certainty of the things in which we have been instructed."

So now here, at the opening of another year of the Church, I call your attention to the undoubted truth announced by St. Luke that the setting forth in order of the things to be believed by a Christian is the way to certainty concerning them.

The fragmentary character of our knowledge, and the lack of order in our thoughts and beliefs concerning Christ, have much to do with the vague impressions and beliefs that obtain respecting His person and His mission. They prevent that firm grasp upon the successive articles of the faith which enables a Christian to stand up against the winds of doctrine that prevail, and amid the waves of doubt which rise up in the mind.

In view of all this it seems strangely objected to this Church of ours, that it is wedded to the observance of days and times which are simply tracing the history on earth of the Saviour of the world. It is loosely supposed that St. Paul in his reflection upon the Jewish observance of "days and times," meant to forestall any such observance by Christians. As though our religion like a piece of machinery were to be regulated according to the clock or the almanac. If you add to this notion the fear of a reliance on these periodical observances as meritorious in themselves, or as leading on, like the days and times of the Jews, to a lapse into formalism, you will account for the prejudice against the days and times of this Church of ours.

The gradual enlightenment of the popular mind has done away with this prejudice, so that at least two of the seasons of the Church commemorative of Christ, to wit, His birth and resurrection, are no longer left floating on the surface of the year, for any considerable body of Christians. These two seasons have been laid hold of throughout Protestant Christendom and placed in their order. It needs no longer a prophet to predict that there they will remain, to give certainty to two important events in which Christians are instructed, to wit, that Christ was born into this world a child, and that as a man He died and rose again. If there is a prejudice more causeless, or a fear of formalism more groundless, than this which for generations has set whole bodies of Christian people against the order of the Christian year,

I am unable to find it. For what is it, if we believe the truth of these words of St. Luke, but a prejudice against being anchored more firmly year by year in the articles of the Christian faith, or a fear of too great a certainty of the things wherein we are instructed.

In order to show the virtue of the Church system to anchor Christians in the faith of the Gospel, and that the idea is founded in the word of God Himself, take the ordinance of the Sabbath day set apart from the beginning of the world to a sacred observance. Unless we are to hold this set time, as excluding all other days and times from the sphere of such observance, then this appointment may fairly be taken as a warrant for other days and times. This Church treats the Lord's day here, as all Christians treat the Lord's prayer, an all sufficient warrant for other prayers.

When we go a step farther as our Saviour did, and say that the sabbath was made for man and not man for the sabbath, we understand that the day was no formal or arbitrary appointment. It had its ample reasons in the welfare of man. It is a needed day of rest for body and mind, a time for lifting our thoughts upward toward God and holy things, and thus furthering our spiritual welfare. In addition to this the sabbath was made a commemorative day.

It was commemorative of a finished creation. It was changed from the seventh to the first day of the week, possibly by Christ's command, and certainly intimated to His Church, by His rising from the dead on that day, by His repeated appearances to His apostles on successive first days of the week, and finally by His choice of that day for the outpouring of His Spirit. The day thus became a commemorative day in the Christian Church. If the Sabbath was appointed as a day of rest from a finished creation, the Lord's day is commemorative of a finished redemption, through the resurrection of our Redeemer from the dead. Under these circumstances, to insist upon the old seventh day of the week, as some who call themselves Christians are still doing, as an immovable day, does seem to question the clear intimation of Christ Himself as Lord of the Sabbath day. Enough on this point.

Now let us look more closely into the virtue there is in the order of the Christian year. It is sadly true that what may be attended to at any time runs the risk of no attention at all. Emphatically true it is of things that have to do with our spiritual interests. It is one of the strongest arguments for the religious observance of this first day of the week. The mass of us may be said to have no time, unless it be set apart for us, for a proper attention to our spiritual needs. With that time given, we are able to overcome a besetting infirmity, and form a habit of attention to our spiritual welfare.

We learn to subordinate the week-day business of our lives to that of the one day of the week thus given to us from heaven. That day comes to arrest the round of our worldly avocations. It comes with its solemn reminders and its religious opportunities. But, and here is the point I have in mind, there is a circle of religious truth. There are the successive facts and events that go to make up our religious faith, and mould our characters and lives. And those facts and events should come round to us in their order of time for a greater certainty and effect.

This day indeed suggests thoughts of a Creator of the world. But it brings up also the thought of a Redeemer of mankind, who rose again from the dead as on this day. There the Lord's day alone, as a guide to thought and a helper to faith, must stop, and leave the subject of it to such serious thoughts as may occur to him. And he drops naturally and almost helplessly into some well-worn rut of thought or feeling, or into one that reaches him in a casual outside way. What therefore is further needed by a devout man or woman, who would make the best use of the sacred day, is a Sunday that will revolve on its axis and show successive phases of Christian truth, and at the same time revolve around the Sun and centre of the Christian system, the person of Christ Himself. In other words we want a Sunday that changes its face, so as to bring out in their order and due proportion the facts and doctrines that complete the circle of what a Christian should believe to his soul's health. This is done for us by the yearly order of this Church. It causes the Lord's day to revolve and bring to view each its different phases of Christian truth.

First of all and beginning with next Sunday it heralds the Advent of Christ in the flesh. It sends us to the prophecies of His first coming to visit us in great humility, and gives us food for meditation in the inspired writings concerning Him of both the Old and New Testaments. The season is long enough to carry our thoughts on to the second coming of Christ in glorious majesty to be our judge, to a consideration of our own latter end, and the last things that are to come upon us, death and the judgment.

As the weeks roll on, its order reveals to us the face of Christ as that of a little child—and His human side comes before us with all its affecting features and surroundings, proving Him to be very man of the virgin Mary His mother.

Anon the child's face gives place to the manifestation of the man, and a man with the power of God. This is the season of the Epiphany, and shews forth the glory of the only begotten of the Father. Then comes to view, slowly but distinctly and impressively, the suffering face of the Son of man, and the Sun of righteousness whose rising has been watched with welcome and with gladness, moves slowly toward His going down.

The Cross appears, first in its dim distance and finally close at hand. The darkness deepens and we begin to count the fearful cost of our redemption. And so we gather strength to renounce the sins that nailed the Saviour to the tree.

Thus the year moves on, lingering where we need to linger, and hastening only at the last, when thus it has prepared us to appreciate the cost of our complete emancipation, and for the final certainty that because He lives we shall live also. It is written in the psalms of a certain day that "This is the day that the Lord hath made, we will rejoice and be glad in it." Measurably that may be said of the Sundays of the year every one in its order.

But the Sunday following the Good Friday of the series, to a member of this Church who follows her as she follows Christ, is emphatically that day. And here let me say that it is not outsiders to the order of the Church who can say with deepest truth, that Easter day is the day that the Lord hath made. For one must first in thought follow Christ through the grave and gate of death, to enter into the joy and gladness of His resurrection. Easter day with no Lenten season and no Good Friday to precede and to prepare us for it, can hardly be more or other religious than any Sunday of the year. Its songs of thanksgiving must lack their uplifting power over us. Its flowers are flowers severed from their root, emblems only of the heart's superficial emotion.

No. It is to disciples of Christ, who like the apostles have been with Him in His temptations and have watched and waited with Him in the garden, at the cross and at the grave that He comes on Easter day as the Sun that illumines a pathway from the sepulchre to the skies, and shines full orbed on the Christian's eternal inheritance. That is the sun that no more goes down, and certifies us that our days of mourning shall be ended.

The songs of such an Easter rise to join with angels and archangels and all the company of heaven, to Him who hath gotten for us the victory. And its flowers are here for tokens of the glory of a life born out of death and the grave.

And now in conclusion, I would put the serious question to men of business and to women cumbered with their cares of this life, even to being jaded at the close of the week, whether, without these Sundays of sacred rest, solemn meditation and devotion, they would have the power, or finally even the inclination to give any appreciable time to the things that belong to their peace.

What a precious boon to them is this day of God,—and what an additional boon is the Church with its order of a year. It saves their being driven hither and thither when the day comes, for a subject or a line of sacred thought. They find one here ready and waiting for them, beginning with next Sunday and stretching along through the weeks and the months that are to follow, all arranged in the order of time, and each occupying its place and asking its share in their Sunday meditations.

I speak here also, not only to men and women with pressing week-day avocations, of the value of the order of this Church.

I speak to people of leisure, with equal anxiety, and especially to the young, of the effect of the Church's system in forming for them a habit of attention to the concerns of the soul—

a habit which will last while life lasts, and help to keep them safely "in the communion of the Catholic Church, in the confidence of a certain faith, and in the comfort of a reasonable religious and holy hope."

May I not add a word of admonition against the loss of a Sunday out of this precious circle of the year?

Men and women before me, bound to labor through the six days, every one of which has its proper work to be done! You feel that you cannot afford to lose one of them and no mere fatigue, no slight indisposition of mind or body, will suffice to keep you from that work.—And shall a Sunday of unpleasant weather find you shut up at home, or a pleasant one find you elsewhere for your ease or pleasure, seeing it is the loss of a Sunday out of your Church's year?

Think first, of what may thus be lost, or if not lost, yet shorn of its freshness and so of some of its virtue or its power over you.

Remember at every recurring temptation or opportunity to let the day and its services go, that they are an added or a brightened link in the chain of the truth as it is in Jesus, and given in order that you may know with ever growing certainty, even to full assurance of those things wherein we have been instructed.

III.

CHRIST'S COMING IN INFANCY—CHRISTMAS.

"The Child Jesus."—St. Luke ii. 43.

THE question of the Saviour Himself to the Jews "What think ye of Christ? Whose son is he?" is a question in one or another of its possible meanings which is still asked and variously answered.

Those who believe Him to be God incarnate, and that is God and man in one person have but one reply to make to this question, "Thou art the Christ the son of the living God." It is the reply of Peter and got for him the singular and distinctive commendation of His master that flesh and blood had not revealed this truth unto him, "but my Father which is in heaven." And yet it was known to Peter and the rest that He had grown up to manhood as the "Child Jesus" born of the virgin Mary. The Child Jesus! and why was the son of the living God born a child? Coming as the second head of the human race, why not as Adam the first head came, whom this same evangelist in tracing the genealogy of the race calls "the son of God"? Certainly, thus coming, He could have commanded the attention of the whole world to His mission and His office. Why, in short, did this Gospel of the Son of God have its apparent root and origin in the infancy of its head?

Does it not occur to us, my brethren, to ask such a question as this? It seems certain that if He had come as a conspicuous and so to speak consummated son of God, such a coming would not only have answered our preconceptions, but would have prevented a thousand doubts and questions and misbeliefs which have prevailed from His day, even down to this, respecting Him. It would have so sharply outlined the dispensation of the gospel that no one could have mistaken it for anything but that which it claims to be, the Gospel of the Son of God.

We can imagine the effect of the advent of such a Christ, clothed with the dignity and authority on earth, ascribed to that type of Him named in the Epistle to the Hebrews as Melchisedec, "without father, without mother, without descent, having neither beginning of days nor end of life, but made like unto the son of God." "Consider, says the writer of this Epistle, how great this man was." Then, indeed, would the Son of God to our conception have come with power. Whereas He did come with scarcely more of human observation than any infant comes on earth. And this is not all. He grew up and passed through the world, even as He came into it, "under the law," subject that is to all the conditions of our humanity till such time as He rose again from the dead. And then at once He disappeared from the eyes of men.

Questions, if we will let them do so, crowd upon us when we endeavor to explain to ourselves or others the life in the flesh of the eternal Son of God; how it was like ours from its beginning to its end on earth tied to other lives, and in well-nigh all the ways our lives are tied up with others; and how those ties were even more bare than ours of all that could give them value by way of social position, wealth, dignity or authority. They did nothing for Him more than for the obscurest among ourselves. Such were His home, His family, His kinsfolk and acquaintance, and all His earthly relations.

Now these questions may be as they have been variously answered, leaving aside all questions of the eternal counsels of God in regard to Him. Leaving them out of our thoughts here also, I ask your attention on this occasion to a reason for the way that Christ came on earth and passed through His earthly life which must come home to us with a wonderful power and to our utter satisfaction. It constitutes the real heartfelt power of His Gospel upon us. The gospel thus viewed will lift men up in spite of themselves whenever it is believed.

I go on to state the reason to which I allude.

Amid the departures and depravities then of man on earth, through four thousand years of time, some things remained that were yet good. Poets have sung of the bliss of Paradise that survived the fall, meaning by it the family ties formed and sanctified in the beginning by God Himself.

The initial tie is that of marriage. This and all that grew out of it, the parental, the filial, the fraternal relations and affections are the remains on earth of man's unfallen condition. They were all here at the coming of Christ with no need that they should be rooted out of our humanity.

The new dispensation could start and go along with marrying and giving in marriage, and with all its innocent results and consequences, to the end of time. Christ born a child is here revealed as condescending to nature, and not as disturbing it. But more.

He used the various relations of life as levers to the uplifting of nature to a higher point. And therefore it was no part of the design of His gospel to change the nature of our domestic life, only to lift it up and pervade it through and through with higher motives and sanctions. Surely nothing could be better calculated to purify the affections of men and to sanctify their domestic and social relations and lead to prizing them at their worth, than that the Son of God should come adopting them for His own, as they had four thousand years before been constituted by His Father in heaven, pure and lovely and of good report.

These pure and innocent relations had become perverted during these ages of the world. It was morally impossible in the course of man's long departure from the innocence of His origin that they should not have become perverted. The love of a child for his father and mother had come to be a calculating affection. It was measured by the standard of an utter selfishness when our Lord declared that the command to honor father and mother had been made void by the traditions of the very people to whom the decalogue was given. And we know also from His own lips with respect to marriage, that Moses was compelled from the hardness of their hearts to suffer a change for the worse in it. From the beginning, our Lord went on to declare, it was not so. The purity of paradise had been lost. And even to this day and in Christian lands it has not been completely recovered, with Christ's own words of the sanctity of marriage ringing in our ears.

Hence the redeeming work of Christ began with the foundations. And a new birth came out of the innocence of Paradise, of the only begotten Son of God, who should cleanse human life at the fountain, sanctify motherhood, lift the whole circle of our domestic affections into an atmosphere of sacredness, and secure for them a profound and lasting reverence.

It must indeed be confessed to be a mysterious advent. An advent which sets at naught all attempts of the wisdom of this world to explain it. And therefore such wisdom will have a Christianity that is free from mysteries. It must have heaven and earth brought together, if at all, in some more striking and convincing way, before it will believe.

And yet, my dear brethren, however mysterious in itself the way of God may appear, I ask you to see how it works with no mystery at all to the redemption and restoration of our humanity to the image of Him who created it; how it lays hold of that humanity, quietly planting in it the germs of its final exaltation.

It is no stumbling-block, how this child born of a woman made under the law redeems them that are under the law, that they may receive the adoption of sons.

What, let me ask, is the design and end of any conceivable relation of God to man? Is it not that of a religion which presents its adequate motives to the purifying and elevating of humanity? which lays hold of every man, woman and child it can reach, with the constraint that makes them new and better men, women and children. And he only is a better man and she a better woman who are more loving, pure and faithful as husbands and wives; and so too the children who love, honor and succor their fathers and mothers, and who never make light of the ties that bind them in filial and fraternal affection. These are the redeemed among men; and little is any religion worth that does not redeem them just here, where they live and move and have their earthly being. Would to God that hard, cold criticism of every kind concerning Christ, as well as persistent unbelief would lay aside the intellectual tools of its trade and look thoughtfully at Him as He lay a child in the arms of His mother, and would let Him get hold of the springs of their own daily and domestic lives. The doubters and the deniers would then find a reason for the Redeemer's advent which, though nothing in the head or the intellect of man suffices to comprehend it, has yet a reason that stirs into life every right instinct of their humanity. Why is it that philosophy has failed, and natural religion has failed, and all the moral maxims that can be brought forward have failed to lift the race of man any higher? It is because none of them have laid hold of the heart of the race. It is because they have neither elevated nor purified the everyday affections of men.

The real tie of human brotherhood has been wanting. Love, yes human love gets its uplifting purifying power from the manger of Bethlehem, where it opened its eyes with all the sympathies of humanity looking out of them, and where it began to take part in the same. The love of a mother for her child, and of the child for its parent, can never be the same to any mother or to any son or daughter after the tidings of this wonderful birth shall have come home to them. It is said and sung of the grave,

"Since Jesus hath lain there I dread not its gloom."

So here with every lowly and innocent thing He touched through life, He touched in order to transform it. He left behind Him in Nazareth what may go on to the end of time making holy the early and the childhood homes of men. The fragrance of His presence in such a home will follow them through life as "a charm from the skies."

This is saving men. It is redeeming them from bondage to the elements of the world and making them sons of God and heirs of eternal life.

Let me speak finally of a misapprehension that has taken possession of not a few people who call themselves Christians.

Because heaven is a place or a condition where there is no marrying, nor giving in marriage, they will have it that all the tender relations of this life are broken off at the grave, and if we are to know one another at all, it will be with these earthly ties gone and forgotten, and in their place something they know not what. Such a heaven may indeed be pure and holy. But where is the warmth or attractiveness in it to a human being? No: Heaven is a character. And the character formed on earth will be a main feature of the heaven above. That character for every one of us will stand there for what it has stood here. It is the result of the relations and associations, affections and aspirations that have made us what we are. And what are we here but husbands and wives, parents and children, brothers and sisters? And the sort of husbands, wives, parents, children and kinsfolk we are here, of that sort we shall be there. That there will be no marrying nor giving in marriage proves only that our heaven is to be invaded by no new relationships. And that is equivalent to saying that the old will survive, and that they shall reappear, never again to be changed or broken. In heaven we shall be like the Child Jesus and like the man. For we shall see Him as He is, "the same yesterday, to-day and forever."

IV.

THE TREE OF LIFE.

"The tree of life also in the midst of the garden."—Genesis ii. 9.

It is very hard to conceive what man was in his created and unfallen condition. Sin has made such ravages with us and with our dwelling place alike, that the present world of nature and of man has only the wreck to show of Adam and the Garden of Eden. There was a brief hour of sunshine and gladness thrown over the scene, and that has not been reproduced on the record so as to give us more than a glimpse of what it was. It is a subject to be approached very humbly and sadly by a Christian, as his childhood's home would be by a long banished man.

The surest guide to the knowledge of what that home was to him, are the instincts which speak for purity and protection and peace and disinterested affection out of his remorseful and longing breast, and the feelings begotten of his experience of the disappointments, the strifes and the weariness of life.

Nevertheless there are truths that come out of the figurative language of this chapter of Genesis well worth pondering for the uses they may serve.

The fall of man is a fundamental article of the Christian faith, because the redemption and restoration of the race through Christ, and that is Christianity, are based upon it.

And we ought to know something of the meaning of the words—"the fall of man." From what did he fall? It is a question that cannot be answered with the certainty that an article of faith requires, unless some definite idea is attached to the spiritual condition of created man, and that idea must be gathered from what is said in this chapter of the Bible. If we pass by this narrative as a myth;—if we put upon its figurative language any meaning we please, or no meaning at all, as best suits our fancy, then the fall of man will be to us a fancy and not a fact.

And just this effect has been wrought upon a large number of people calling themselves Christians. Regarding the narrative before us as too mythical or obscure for founding any doctrine of religion upon it, or, having theories of religion inconsistent with any fair interpretation of the narrative, makes the fall of man a fancy or a myth, or if a fact, one without any influence in their theology. The Garden of Eden stands in their Bibles a pretty picture with a dark background, but one at which none of them anxiously looks to see man either as he was in the beginning, is now, or ever shall be.

The first chapter of this book, as is well known, has to be interpreted in the light of natural science, and to some not very clear intellects it seems not only a new reading, but a contradiction of Scripture. And so their faith is small in the narrative of the second chapter, and possibly in all the rest. At least we may say that for many the whole foundation of Scripture has been shaken. This account of the origin of man and his created estate, and his fall therefrom, is among the first to be dismissed out of the account of things either to be acted upon or credited.

Again:—There is a strong drift in our times toward ridding Christianity of all definiteness and all visible embodiment. Both these are regarded as trammels upon the individual, and the sooner he gets rid of them the more rapidly he will develop the Godlikeness and the humanity that are in him. Such preaching as this goes on to-day in pulpits and to people calling themselves Christians. I do not know that it would change the character of such preaching were preachers and hearers both convinced that the sort of religion prescribed by the Almighty God to His unfallen creatures, had in it both these, to them, outgrown elements, to wit:—a clearly defined faith, and an outward organization; in other words, a creed and a Church.

But it may help us who still hold to these things, to prize them at their worth, when we discover that for man unfallen and sinless, as well as for his fallen descendants, neither creed nor church was dispensed with. It will go hard with any so-called law of progress in the human race ere it reaches as high a point of privilege or freedom as Adam occupied in Paradise. What of outward help was not dispensed with *there*, no man can be charged with folly in refusing to let go to the latest or brightest day that is yet to dawn on the earth that now is.

Let us not, on the one hand, indulge in unavailing regrets that we have lost our birthright, or on the other deem the inquiry a useless one which may bring some features of it before our minds. Let us bear in mind that the reality of the inheritance we were made for is yet, thanks be to God, through Jesus Christ, in reserve for all who love Him.

One of the features then that belonged to

our birth-spot was the tree of life. It was the central figure in the home of our first parents —"in the midst of the garden." It was not there to embellish a lovely scene or add variety to its products. Like another tree there, it had a meaning beyond this. It was no mere means of sustaining the animal life;—all were trees of life in this lower sense of the word, being pleasant to the sight and good for food,—while this only was called the tree of life. This tree was afterward hedged round in a miraculous manner, so that fallen man could not reach it. The inference is that he had not eaten of it. What would have befallen had he done so, we do not know, nor need we speculate.

But the point which seems proved by the existence of this tree and by what is said of it, is this:—that man had not in possession when created, all that was necessary to his happy immortality. A part thereof rested in promise of which this tree was a token and pledge. With the animal life and the means to sustain it actually and amply bestowed, there was a promise also given to man of eternal life, and that promise was betokened to him by the tree in the midst of the garden. The act of eating of that tree was to be no mere animal act, or for the sake of gratifying an appetite. It was a sacramental act,—an act of faith,—an act of religion,—a laying hold, so to speak, of the covenant of immortality which God made with a being created out of the dust of the earth, and who without something more done for him would have gone back to dust. This conclusion cannot be avoided if you give any special meaning, whether figurative or literal, to this tree.

Let us look now for a moment at the nature of created and unfallen man which made this act of faith needful or proper. He had certain gifts and endowments which his fall did not touch, and in those he was the same then as he is now. He had a body with its appetites and passions and susceptibilities, and he had a rational mind and a will, with the power to choose. All these he still has. But over and above these were superadded what we may call supernatural and spiritual gifts, enabling him to stand upright and sinless. These made him a religious being, as the others made him an animal and an intellectual being. And these are the gifts that the fall affected. It did not blot them out, but it disturbed them ;—it weakened them.—It, so to speak, upset them. It left the religious susceptibilities in him, but it left him without the power to waken or to impress them, or to set those faculties to work; and that is our case now.

Had he not fallen,—here then was room and office for the tree of life. Adam, unendowed by nature with eternal life, but depending on the grace of God for it, was to receive that grace in an appointed way, so that man unfallen relied, as man fallen and redeemed relies, upon a divine promise. And the tree of life whatever it was outwardly or in itself, was to him a sacrament of spiritual and eternal life,—a means whereby he was to receive the same and a pledge to assure him thereof.

This covenant which God made with unfallen man, sealed and betokened to him by the fruit of the tree of life, was broken by an act of wilful disobedience on his part. Broken on one side, it was treated as broken on all sides, and the promise of God in it withdrawn. Hence the flaming sword. Meaning that the promise was lifted away out of human reach, with all the tokens and signs that belonged to it. Eternal life, we may say, then disappeared in the form under which it had been offered. Man, having chosen death rather than life, death was given to him accordingly.

And now it is literally through death that he must reach life eternal. It is a roundabout way that we are now to take. That we can reach it at all is owing to God's mercy in providing at His own great cost, a death through which we may pass to the gates of everlasting life. The sacrament of unfallen man was a tree of life:—that of man fallen and redeemed has a death in it as the source of its virtue. And the entire surroundings of human probation have undergone a corresponding change. The easy way to glory and honor and immortality to unfallen man was through a garden of delights and a tree in the midst of it, of which he might have eaten and lived forever. To man fallen is given an outside waste of thorns and thistles, labor and travail, and the gate of death. Let me say that the account given in Scripture of the creation and fall of man, the Garden of Eden and the tree of life, together with the analogy of this faith, corroborated and sustained by catholic tradition and consent, make such to be the heritage from which we fell and such the fall of man.

When we say that man was made perfect we ought to understand what that perfection means. If by it we suppose that he had in possession, or by right, or within his power by virtue of his creation, all that he necessarily required for his continued uprightness and happiness, we are mistaken. It is a mistake which will lead, if it has not already led, to the idea of the recuperative power of human nature, and the inherent capability of the race of man to develop itself to all imaginable perfection. It is a notion that takes man, not as he was when God made him, but as he is in his fall or his depravity, or perversity, without any further gift of God than he is blest with as he comes into the world, his education, civilization and what not, and supposes him able to save himself and make progress toward all imaginable good. If it takes the fall into the account, it does so not as having caused an inheritable and an inherited spiritual lack or distortion in human nature, but as a something that happened to the head of a family six thousand years ago, and which has long since exhausted all its baneful consequences. It finds among the fragments of the fall everything needful to a reconstruction of man in the image of Him that created him. It finds the spiritual eye in him neither blinded nor distorted out of the power of education to remedy. It finds the ear to hear and the heart to understand.

In answer to all this, we say it is what man never had, save by the superadded grace of God. If the advocates of the idea say that the fall is a myth and there is no such thing as original sin, I answer, let it be a myth, and then there never was such a thing in man as inherent and original righteousness. It was imparted to him as a favor by the Almighty. It was a gift of grace, and he was tied to divine ordinances in order to secure it.

If there had been no fall, or supposing there has been none, then man in his progress toward perfection as a religious being, was, from the beginning, a dependent on the grace of God. He was to seek it as a suppliant from His bounty, in the use of sacraments and ordinances and means of grace. He was a creature that might fall in a moment, and without these appointed helps from God would fall as he did, and debase the image of his Maker. The idea that means of grace may be dispensed with as elements of spiritual life and growth in a human being or the human race—that embodied Christianity is nothing, with its sacraments and ordinances and worship, and that God's external appointments are or may safely be superseded by man's obedience to his conscience, or the law that is in him, by whatever name it goes, is an idea that more than sets aside the doctrine of natural depravity. It makes man a better and a stronger creature than he was created.

God only knows how far the notion that is getting hold of people, that there is no inherited or natural spiritual helplessness in human beings, is to be carried. Certain it is, that it is the great religious error a Christian has to combat and resist in these days; and if the name of Jesus Christ did not stand forth so prominently, and in Scriptures that are not yet scouted or cast overboard, I should fear that He would be put to an open shame. As yet His Name is acknowledged, even by those who leave Him nothing to do on earth. To them His atonement is nothing; His church and sacraments are nothing, while His example, if it is held up for imitation is used among other mere persuasives to a moral life.

And why should it be otherwise if there was no fall of man? There is logic in it. If the second chapter of Genesis discloses no truth in which all the descendants of Adam are involved; and if the third chapter does not bring to light the fact that man was lost beyond his unassisted power to recover himself, then what are the writings of the four Evangelists worth? The Son of man came to seek and to save that which was lost. If it was not lost in Paradise, then it never has been lost; and that, substantially, is the ground that is taken. And it is taken because men do not know what loss is when it comes to the soul and the spirit within them. Such loss is the severance of that soul from God. It is a loss to be spiritually discovered, and it needs the Spirit of God and the law of God, brought in contact with the human conscience before the impassable gulf appears between man and his Maker.

There is a human standard of righteousness and innocence that has been substituted for that which is a discerner of the thoughts and intents of the heart. And by that the moral worth of human nature has been tried and not found wanting. It may not be the low standard of the market place;—it is a little better. But it is what every man and woman can reach who will live a little better and try to reach. The preaching and the practising of such a religion might be tolerated by a Christian, if it were not done under the pretense of its being the Christian religion. For, though it may lack adequate motive, to the answering of even its moderate demands, it pitches the goal of perfection ever a little farther on than men have attained,—and so far it is good for the temporal well-being of society. But it is not the religion of the Bible nor the religion of the gospels, and the sooner we understand that it does not touch the weak spot that God sees in us, the more likely are we to discard it from our hopes forever. What He has made provision for, and what He demands, is the knitting again of the severed tie of Paradise. Without that, to Him we are dead, as was Adam when he snapped the thread in twain that bound him to his Maker.

And the religion which is to bind his descendants back is not a mere religion of decent living, every one according to his light, however smoothly the reciprocal affections we have for one another may be playing their part. It is a religion that first and foremost draws the soul toward God and then draws the souls of men together. It works to that end through ordinances, as it offered to keep unfallen man tied to his Maker. To man fallen is offered still the tree of life. It stands, though unseen, in His Church which is the substitute in the world to-day for the Eden we have lost. Organized and embodied religion is here as the means whereby lost man is to be saved. It is here as a daily reminder,—as a token of the covenant of God with man,—as the promise that is left us of entering into His rest,—as a means whereby we may, though in the world, be living above it and feeding while here on the food of immortality.

For that Tree is Christ, who died and is risen again and is head over all things to the Church which is His body.

V.

POPULAR PREJUDICES AGAINST THE GOSPELS.

"And they were offended in Him. But Jesus said, a prophet is not without honor save in his own country and in his own house."

"And He did not many mighty works there because of their unbelief.—St. Matt. xiii. 57, 58."

THERE is an important truth implied in this passage of Scripture. Encountering a state of unbelief our Saviour ceased His labors among a people, when we should have expected Him to go on with His endeavors to convince them of His divine mission.

St. Mark adds to the incident here recorded by St. Matthew that He marveled because of their unbelief.

The inference is that He had said and done enough to show that He was all He had claimed to be, and that His doctrine was the truth of God. And in that case it was time thrown away to labor further among a people whose mere wilfulness or perversity lay at the bottom of their rejection of Him.

The important truth I refer to, then, is that

religious unbelief is largely a wilful, rather than an involuntary state of a sound mind.

It depends rather upon what is in the power of a sane man's will, whether he believes the truth or not. And that is the fault of his prepossessions, prejudices or inclinations. For these he will be held responsible. If under their influence he will not believe the truth, whose sufficient evidence is before him, he is justly answerable for his unbelief, and he will be left as our Lord here left the people that were offended in Him, to the consequences of his wilful rejection of the truth.

It may prove a startling discovery to men who affect to think, so they often say, that their religious belief is not under their control, and if they do not believe it is because they cannot. Such persons will deny the inference we draw from the treatment by our Lord of the unbelief of His day. And all the more will they be inclined to reject the Christianity which they think they cannot accept, when they find charged upon them such a responsibility as this.

Certainly no man can fairly be held responsible for the innate weakness or obliquity, or the slowness of his intellectual perceptions, and the helpless constitution of his mind.

If we can fairly impute his unbelief to this,

we can be sure that it will be mercifully dealt with by the Judge of all the earth. But he is responsible for letting his prepossessions, preconceptions and prejudices get the better of the power of discernment that God has given him.

He is, according to the passage before us, responsible for his prejudices against the person through whom, or his dislike for the mode by which, the truth offers to reach him. He can part with these mere likes and dislikes or leave them altogether out of his thoughts, if he will, and so come to a proper state of mind for reaching the truth. If on the other hand his prejudices are dearer to him than the truth, he will hold on to them and let the truth go. He will not merely let it go. He will not believe it. He will reject it. Human nature is a perverse and curious compound. It often takes the simple obstinacy of its will, for the conclusions of its judgment, and rests easy under what is seen by others to be a transparent self-deception. And marvelous indeed it is to find so many people, sensible and reasonable in other respects, rejecting and resisting the most concerning of all possible truth. Such, however, was the treatment accorded to the Gospel and its Divine author when they came into the world, and such it is down to this day. Such, at this moment it may be, with some before me.

I would if possible on this occasion get at some part of what I may call the wilfulness of our day, on the important subject of religion; the likes and dislikes that stand in the way of a ready and a hearty acceptance of the truth as it is in Jesus Christ. And I would convince such unbelievers if I can, with God's help, that they must yield their cherished notions, their mere wishes and their preferences, if they would save their souls.

Here, for a first illustration of the wilfulness to which I refer, is one who does not like the doctrine of everlasting punishment. He sees no justice in such a doom for any human being. And he will not accept a religion or join a church which has any such teaching in it, or which allows any portion of mankind to perish forever. Now, without going into the large and complex question of what future punishment is—how, if at all, it differs from the inevitable reaping hereafter of what a man sows here, let me say that the worst and darkest side of this doctrine according to the Scriptures, makes future punishment only a future contingency. The Gospel of Christ does not contemplate the damnation of men. On the contrary it is a gospel of salvation from it. It shows the way to escape it. And it is a way open and accessible to all men. That is the Gospel which we are set here to preach. And the fear of hell is no proper motive of that Gospel. Its moving power over us is the redeeming love of Christ. And therefore do I say that the deepest rooted dislike of this doctrine need not stand one moment in the way of any one's becoming a Christian. No man is required to believe it of himself. On the contrary, to be a Christian is to be emancipated at once and forever from all fear of future punishment. Nor need he believe it of his neighbors. By the character he assumes in becoming a Christian, he is forbidden to judge his fellow men. Not only vengeance belongeth unto God, but all judgment and with Him our religion of Charity and good-will to men bind us to leave it. It follows that you who dislike this doctrine, may if you will, all the more easily embrace the essential and merciful truths of the Gospel, which steer altogether clear of it. If a sinner should come to me with the question uppermost in his mind how he should escape future torment, I should say to him that his heart was not right. And I should strive by dilating on the redeeming love of Christ to drive that fear out of his bosom. I should say to him "The fear of hell's a hangman's whip," and not a weapon that God has put into my hands.

I am placed here not to drive men, but to

persuade them; not to threaten with future perdition, but "To allure to brighter worlds and lead the way." I pray you who have put this stumbling-block in your way to loosen your hold on it, so far as to look the loving, constraining and saving truths of Christianity in the face, till, if you have to confess that there is in it the thing you dislike, that there is also a love there, and a pity and a constraint beyond all you have thought or dreamed. And these make the fact of a future hell of no concern or consequence to you. What if there be a hell if there be none for you, or for any man who will flee to lay hold of the hope set before him in the Gospel?

Conquer your prejudice against the religion of Christ here, by contemplating the heaven of eternal blessedness brought to light in the Gospel. And so turn your dislikes into so many reasons for being a Christian, and for proclaiming to the world around you that there is indeed no hell, and no condemnation to them who are in Christ Jesus.

Another very common prejudice against our religion is a dislike for its forms and sacraments, and its supposed exclusiveness. This seems a growing dislike at the present day. Religion is regarded as limiting its blessings and privileges to those who become through these ceremonies, members of the Church. And so people dislike what they deem its exclusiveness. They will not place themselves in a position in which, through mere forms which have no virtue in themselves, they are to be counted holier than other men, or better Christians than many of their neighbors, who have as much Christlikeness as they have, and as they will humbly think, even more. There is a great deal of this mistaken sensitiveness and affected humility to be met with.

It keeps some people from attendance upon religious observances, and even from keeping the Lord's day in a religious manner. And these are the lowest and least conspicuous among the forms of our religion. It is carrying dislike to an extreme. But there is assumed to be a principle involved in it and therefore people do it. They found their dislike for forms in their own greater liberality, toleration and charity than those of the Church, for views and practices that differ from it. They prefer not to narrow themselves, as they think they would, by adopting the Church view of the Christian religion. And so they stand aloof from the things that are distinctive of it before the world.

Let me put this one question to such people. How long do they suppose Christianity would last in the world if this dislike of theirs were to have its way? Let the things about religion that they dislike or consider non-essential be done away with, and what would be left? How long would the spirit of Christianity which they like, outlast the body of it which they dislike?

Suppose church-going to cease; suppose the religious observance of the Lord's day to come to an end, to say nothing of letting go the sacraments of the Gospel? And you need not suppose anything further in order to wipe out of the land not the body only but the soul of Christianity in less than fifty years. The lifetime of one generation would do it effectually. Ponder this one truth, that you cannot educate, instruct or impress religiously, without forms, and I mean visible signs, symbols and memorials of religious truth. You cannot keep religion alive in the hearts of men without statedly and recurring times and significant ways of renewing its impressions upon the mind. And if the true Christian spirit, which is the spirit of Christ, is to be kept alive in the breasts of His followers, what He said and what He did on earth by way of impressing it upon them, must be kept in their remembrance. It must be brought before their eyes from time to time for this purpose. If the spirit of sacrifice is to live and grow in the minds of men, then the great sacrifice of Christ's death on Calvary must come to the front of their remembrance, and be set forth before their eyes, that the spirit of Christ may enter and be kept alive in selfish breasts.

Now, what men like in the Christian religion is the unselfish spirit they find there, and its fruits in the lives of His followers. What they dislike in it is its outward forms, its observances, public and private, its sacraments and memorials. But they cannot have what they like, or they cannot keep and preserve it, unless they also take and keep and cherish what they dislike.

What will they do? There are growing numbers who will not take the first step toward securing and perpetuating pure and undefiled religion on the earth which they confess to be their heart's desire, and which they may do by simply and openly joining the Church, because that first step is one they dislike to take. No harm comes to themselves from that step; no compromise of conscience or principle is required of them, and no injustice is done to any human being. Neither is there anything intolerant or uncharitable or exclusive in it. It is a delusion with which conscientious men and women seek to reconcile themselves to the neglect of the plainest duty they owe to God and their neighbors.

PREJUDICES AGAINST THE GOSPELS. 61

Where do they get the idea of the exclusiveness of the Church? Its doors are open to all believers. Its Creeds are a simple rehearsal of the facts of Christianity which they believe already, if they accept Christianity at all. And let me add, that a man's open confession of Christ constitutes a rebuke to his non-Christian friend and neighbor, which he is bound to administer. Charity itself requires it. And it is a rebuke which in nine cases out of ten would be heeded.

Men of standing and weight in the community, often set the example of rejecting the forms and sacraments of Christ's religion. Every one of them who overcomes his dislike for these things so far as to adopt them, no longer blocks the way of his neighbors to them, and he escapes, as no otherwise he can escape, the woe pronounced by the Author of our religion upon those "who enter not in themselves and them that were ready to enter they hinder." May God forgive them for casting the weight of their characters against the cause of Christ through the indulgence of their likes and dislikes.

Another obstacle which people are letting stand in the way of their salvation, is a dislike for mysteries in religion. They dislike, as they say, to be blindly led. They want to see all clear and comprehensible in the way they are to take, and in the things they are to believe. It makes no difference to them how much in religion is made plain and comprehensible, as the whole of it is that requires anything to be done, even by a child. If there were anything doubtful or mysterious here, there might be a reason for disliking and objecting. But because the Incarnation is a mystery, or the Atonement is a mystery, or because the doctrine of the Trinity is a mystery; all mysteries, mind you, with which God and not man is chiefly concerned, men will not repent of their sins, nor be baptized for the remission of them, nor will they believe in Christ, nor keep His commandments, which are no mysteries at all.

Yes: Here is a means divinely wrought out for a sinner's reconciliation unto God. It is let down we may say from heaven to earth. It is like a rope thrown to a drowning man. But because he cannot understand just how it is held or fastened at its upper end, he will not lay hold of it. He has every reason for believing that it is let down by a friendly hand, and will answer his purpose. But so long as there is anything about it that he cannot understand, he refuses to avail himself of it.

And so the man prefers to have no hope and be without God in the world, rather than part with his dislike for the mystery in which it pleases that great Being to shroud Himself, His works and ways. This is worse than mere wilfulness. It is madness. And yet it is the wilfulness and the madness of a finite being, to whom religion has become a stumbling-block because he cannot understand the infinite God. The religion of Christ is really the person of Christ and He is the mystic ladder whose top is in heaven.

How it rests or is held there, or how He is Divine, being a man, is hidden from human sight. We do not know nor can we from the nature of the case. We who find earthly things often hard to understand, how can we understand the heavenly? But the bottom of that ladder is the entire humanity of Christ and rests upon the solid earth appealing to every man to test its virtue.

And yet there are those who will let their dislike for the mystery about it, that cannot possibly be helped, stand forever in the way of their laying hold on the hope set before them.

Other likes and dislikes there are which are stumbling-blocks to believing. One more only will I name without dwelling upon it. And that is a dislike for the inconsistencies of Christians. Instead of this being allowed to keep men from being Christians it ought to bring them into the Church. They know what religion requires. And if they fail to discover it in Christians round about them, surely the plainest dictates of duty bid them step forth and show what it is by their own consistent lives. This is what they would inevitably do, if their regard for the honor of religion were as near their hearts as it seems to be from their strong dislike for Christian inconsistency. But I will go no further on this occasion in the endeavor to unmask the various excuses for unbelief. I have alluded to such of them as seem to have some show of reason, and to be the most prevalent among us.

I would close what I have to say to those who make these excuses, or who put forth any other, for standing aloof from the religion of Christ, by asking them to ponder this one assurance of Christ Himself that "God so loved the world that He gave His only begotten Son that all that believe in Him should not perish but come to everlasting life."

I beg them hereafter to look to Him, in whom is no fault at all, and see in the bright light of His example of life, His death and sacrifice for the sins of the world, how trivial becomes the whole legion of excuses for not closing with the terms of His Gospel. I ask them to see how His majestic character, His redeeming love, His suffering life and His atoning death dwarf into shame their little subterfuges and scatter their excuses to the winds.

The mere thought, when you shall have done with the things of this world and are brought face to face before Him, of what has stood, perhaps for a lifetime as a stumbling-block in your way of believing on Him, will leave you speechless. To have let a notion, a prejudice, a caprice empty the love of Christ of all its constraining power over you, will be a marvel hereafter equal to its madness and folly.

God forbid it to every soul before me this day.

VI.

THE PRAYER OF THE SYRO-PHENICIAN WOMAN.

"Then came she and worshipped Him saying, Lord help me."—St. Matt. xv. 25.

THIS Gospel records the working of a deeply felt need in the heart of a human being. It was not only a deeply felt need, but on a human calculation, a desperate one. Its effect was one of those wearing wounds of the heart that will only be relieved when the cause is gone. That which was agonizing to this poor mother was worse than death, because it was a daily and an hourly laceration of her maternal feelings to have to look at her daughter with the light of reason and intelligence gone out of her eyes. If there is such a thing as the torture of a living death, then was that torture here; not in the victim, blessed be God for His mercy. It is the one solace that the real sufferers, the friends of such a human wreck can have. The wreck itself is too great for the subject of it to know how great it is. And so the need of this mother broke forth in the prayer, rather for herself than for her daughter, "Lord help me."

The case suggests as a subject of discourse, Prayer. And I will endeavor to treat it in its successive steps as they appear in this gospel story.

In the first place notice who the woman was. She was a Greek, and therefore to the Jews, a heathen woman. She belonged to a stock which put her farther from the true God than the ordinary heathen were. She was a woman of Canaan. She belonged to a tribe of people doomed for their sins to extirpation. She had no clear sense of her spiritual condition and wants. Her needs were those only of our common humanity. The pressure upon her was simply that of suffering maternal affection, an instinct of nature. And that tells us plainly enough that prayor is also such an instinct. The cry of a human soul to God is just as natural in its sufferings and privations as the craving of human love. The one goes out as naturally toward a Supreme Being as the other goes out toward human beings. And the only needful explanation of this truth is that so God made us.

Volumes may be written, as perhaps they have been, to prove the uselessness of prayer to God; to prove of that unchangeable Being that He must change before prayer can be effectual, or that the laws of nature must be changed.

In answer to all that has been or can be written in this direction, we may say that Prayer is also a law of nature, and that it is as impossible to change the human constitution as the Divine will. What is to be said of such a deadlock as this appears to be, between the different laws of the same God, between the laws impressed upon the soul of man and those which are impressed upon the face of nature? If prayer is a worthless exercise, then why was the instinct of prayer inserted into the constitution of the human being? The question cannot be answered to the forbidding or repressing of prayer when prompted by human suffering and privation.

Why then attempt to answer it at all? It is treading, to say the least, on the mysterious border ground between the soul of man and the Maker of that soul. And in treading there, cold philosophy is treading human instincts and affections and aching hearts under foot. It is ground which it were a thousand times better to let alone, than to touch with the weight of an argument or a reason or a question.

Secondly:—Notice the power of this instinct,

and that is the power of prayer to overcome difficulties in its path.

This woman had no special claim to the favor or the attention of Him to whom she made the appeal. She found herself at the first step in an unfamiliar region and in strange and unfriendly association. The experience was new to her. She sent her petition out of the coasts of her own country, if haply it might reach the ear of Him to whom she cried. There was no sign sent back that He had even listened to it. "He answered her not a word." That looks like a vast many of our prayers. They do not seem to reach their destination. They fall back dead upon our souls. And then we incline to stop and ask where is the profit? This woman is an example to all such, that they do not draw back nor stop with any thought like that. Prayer is not like smiting a rock and then going our ways. It is not smiting the rock at a distance and then waiting even expectingly for the water to come forth. The real prayer follows itself up without waiting.

Here was a prayer too, seconded by the prayers of others. "Lord send her away," that is, grant her request and send her away.

Others touched by sympathy with our wants join their prayers with ours. It is an encouragement to go on with our own, and an encouragement that we need. But here, though evidently encouraged by the request of the disciples, there came back to the woman a sign such as we should be inclined to take as one of simple and final refusal.

From answering to the first cry of the woman not a word, came this answer of Christ to the prayer of the disciples for her, "I am not sent but to the lost sheep of the house of Israel."

And so we often think, that not being among the favored people of God and not His accepted children, but strangers to Him, perhaps conscious sinners against Him, we have little hope that we shall be heard. And so we wait till we can have some ground for hope.

In such a condition, or under the influence of such feelings, many never become believers in Christ at all, because they never pray at all. They make no nearer approach to the exercise than an occasional longing under the urgency of some of their many needs, that He would help them. Hardly is such a longing prayer. It is but the prompter to prayer. Let the prayerless who are in trouble follow the example of this woman!

She had nothing to commend her to the Saviour of the world but her needs as a human being. She was the mother of a child in sore need, and whatever else she was, the sequel proved that to be enough. "Then," it is said, "she came and worshipped Him"; then, when to her prayer He had answered not a word, and to the prayer of His disciples for her He gave a reason why her prayer should not be granted. To her it was a reason for going on and breaking the barrier down between chosen people and strangers. She would not be a stranger any longer, if a worshipper of Him could be counted as a disciple or a friend.

My dear friends, who have been deterred from approaching in prayer this Saviour of the world, on the ground of your alienage or your unworthiness, what do you think of the power of prayer, without reference to the answer of God to it, to break that alienage down, and turn a stranger into a worshipper of the true God?

As Christians, we fain look to God for a demonstration of the power of prayer, and look for it in some palpable answer of the Almighty to our poor petitions. And I do not deny that we may sometimes, or eventually, find it there. But the true place to look for it, is in its reactive effect upon ourselves. Without an answer, without a word or a favorable sign, and without signs to the contrary, prayer will remove mountains. It will level the difficulties in a sinner's way to Christ. It will bring him face to face with that all-merciful and all-powerful Being, pleading with Him as a man pleads with his friend. The special answer to prayer may lie farther on. It may come or it may not come. The efficacy of prayer you cannot doubt in the face of this miracle of the woman of Canaan. It has the power to bring us unto God. It has the power to draw us nigh to God, which He makes the one condition of His drawing nigh to us.

I beg every far-off man and woman and every cold-hearted Christian among you, by prayer to put that promise to the test, and thus to shorten the distance between themselves and God. Herein the text is your warrant and your example. Follow it and you will not doubt again whether prayer is an unmeaning or a profitless service.

In one more step let us follow the story of the woman of Canaan. She is at last on her knees a worshipper of Christ, and brought there by the power of prayer, hindered though she was at every step of her drawing nigh. And then for the first time He breaks the silence on His side. By that token, intercourse is established between them, even according to His promise to such.

But what is the reply He makes? Let us look to that, for we are deeply concerned with

PRAYER OF SYRO-PHENICIAN WOMAN. 73

it, we who are looking to God for a favorable answer to our prayers. His reply seemed to make matters worse than His silence. "It is not meet to take the children's bread and cast it to dogs." Here is delay and apparent denial.

So too it often is with us, who go as far as this, and then yield to disheartening signs that settle like a chill upon our souls. We let them take away the ground on which we stand, and conclude that we have asked amiss. We think as this woman might have thought, that we are not deemed worthy of the blessing we ask and let go our hold on God who is really listening to us. Prayer can hardly go on to good effect under feelings like these. The beginning of faith will fail, and the danger is lest we be cast back farther than we were at first from our hope in God that He will hear us.

The example of the woman of Canaan tells us what in such a case to do. Let us ponder the signs and indications of God's will. Often is there a hidden yea under the apparent nay of the merciful Hearer of our prayers, if we would only look for it. We fervently deprecate a pressing or a threatened evil. It threatens still. It comes nearer day by day till it is upon us. What shall we do? Shall we give over our prayers against it and let it come with all its paralyzing power, endeavoring perhaps in vain to say "Thy will be done"?

That is prayer fallen to the ground, and possibly we miss some better thing than we have asked, hidden under the delay or the denial. Let me take a not uncommon case, one like this mother's. Death threatens her child. Prayer for the life of that child is as instinctive as the instinct of life itself. And yet the signs and indications are all against granting the prayer. Accepting them on their face and letting them come without a further struggle with Him in whose hand life is, is what we too often do. Accepting them and yet struggling on marked the prayer of the woman of Canaan. And her prayer He granted. He has done it often. The Psalmist speaks of such a case, perhaps his own for his child that nevertheless died. "He asked life of thee and thou gavest it him, and the life granted was length of days forever and ever."

Here is the prayer of faith, the praying and the fainting not. It is the example of Jacob, "I will not let thee go except thou bless me." Such is the example of the woman of Canaan. Her persevering faith saved herself as well as her daughter. For small was the boon she asked, compared with that which by prayer she finally obtained. Here were two strangers found sitting at the feet of Jesus, clothed and in their right minds, the mother obtaining for herself more than she either desired or deserved. Let us learn from this, that there is something higher and better in prayer than the mere obtaining of our shortsighted petitions.

There is apparent harshness in the utter silence of Christ under cries that touched the hearts of His disciples. There was apparent strangeness in Him on that occasion to the wants and woes of our humanity. And these signs appear all around us in the privations and miseries of our fellow creatures, innocent themselves of all wrong, suffering at times to torture of body or of soul under the afflictions as it were of God's Providence. It is a hard chapter on the face of it to read that yet we are compelled to read by daily observation and experience. But we ought to know that things are not what they seem. The end of them is what shall best characterize them. The blessings that lie under them will come out at last and shew the mercy of God. What brings out those blessings, is the silent and expectant waiting upon God with a holy and a humble trust in Him. And we need that most of all amid the miseries of the world we live in.

He will answer prayer when its work is done of drawing us nigh to God, its work of increasing our faith in and our reliance upon Him.

Then it will be unto us as we will; not always because the passionate wish of our hearts, with which we began it, is granted, but because there comes over us in the end a calm, unwavering trust in God which reaches its height in enabling us cheerfully to say, "Thy will be done." Such, let us always remember, was the end of the Saviour's own prayer in the garden.

My dear brethren, I have endeavored to show you the profit of prayer. I have tried to discover from this miracle of Christ how prayer works upon ourselves to bring us to God and how it works to bring Him unto us. All this stands out step by step and clearly in the case of the woman of Canaan.

And I ask you to confess this to be one chief virtue of the exercise. What boon can be greater than that which thus we obtain, whether or not we obtain the petitions which we ask of God. If our wants and privations grow less severe and more tolerable under the exercise, then are the pressure and suffering which prompt to prayer gone out of a troubled spirit. Better it is for us, and we often live to see it, that our wishes are not granted; better that they should be changed as they are changed by prayer, and the communion that follows with our God.

Here indeed He wrought a miracle in answer

to an earnest prayer. That is our warrant for the hope that He may come to us in the way we ask. But the great mercy is, that prayer will surely bring us unto God. By it we may surely keep the command to which is attached the richest boon ever offered to sinful, burdened souls on earth:—

"Come unto me and I will give you," possibly not what you ask, but I will give you what you need, "rest unto your souls."

VII.

FASTING FOR CHRIST'S SAKE.

"But the days will come when the bridegroom shall be taken away from them, and then they shall fast in those days."—St. Mark ii. 20.

THE season of Lent is regarded by many as a mere Church appointment, and if it were nothing more they ought to keep it, in acknowledgment of the authority of the Church to appoint holy seasons and to prescribe the mode of their observance. But fasting,—and I use the word in its larger sense, not only of abstinence from feasting and the delicacies of the table, but from the social companies, pleasures and amusements of other times,—is not a mere Church appointment, nor does it rest for its highest authority or sanction on immemorial church custom or tradition. We are told there is no warrant in the New Testament for the keeping of Lent, and that fasting is not obligatory upon Christians. It is a mistake. If directions as to the manner of fasting have any meaning, they mean to let us know how we should discharge an undoubted religious duty.

They who observe the season of Lent from no other reason than that it is a Church appointment, will take the liberty of observing it in their own way, or in a way they think most conducive to their own good. I fear that such people have not given it enough of consideration,—for there is to careful and devout readers of the New Testament, and to those who give their thoughts to the scope and design of this forty days, more in it than they have supposed. What do they think, for example, of the words of the present text?—that "the days come when the Bridegroom is to be taken away" and that "then shall they fast in those days." They may not regard it as a bidding to fast or an ordinance of Christ, in so many words. But if they are not as the horse and mule that must be governed by the bit and bridle of a "Thus saith the Lord";—if, as docile and obedient children of the Bridegroom, they are willing to be guided by His wishes and His intimations,—then have they here a touching intimation of His will. It is in the shape of a reminder and a prediction as respects His followers. He declared that while He was with them, they would not fast,—not that they need not or must not, but that the fitness of things, which at one time forbids, at another demands fasting. Is not this what the passage fairly implies? And then you will not let this intimation of the will of Christ be exhausted upon the persons of those to whom He gave it, but you will accept these words as meaning something to you who read them now. " Watch and pray lest ye enter into temptation." This the first disciples were bidden to do, when their Lord was taken from them to His death. They did it again between the day of His ascension into heaven and the descent of the Holy Ghost on the day of Pentecost. But was this all He meant by the Bridegroom's being taken away? Not if we are also the children of the Bridegroom, and not if we are part of the Church which is the spouse and bride of the Lord Jesus Christ.

There are seasons when we may be said to have Him with us even as the disciples of old, —the season of His advent on earth and of His resurrection from the dead and all along His earthly life as we trace it through His epiphany, His childhood, His manhood, His active ministry. All these have their proper thoughts and associations according to the yearly round of this Church. Thus we have our seasons when the Bridegroom may be said to be with us. Some of them are seasons of rejoicing, even of feasting and social pleasure, and who will dare to say that this passage of Scripture which speaks of the presence of the Bridegroom, has no reference whatever to these commemorative seasons, or that it did not contemplate the state of things that exists in His Church to-day? If it did not, then the fitness of things which He contemplated in the rejoicing of His disciples is no fitness for us. It never can happen again and there is nothing that answers to it now on earth. You cannot help believing that this prediction or intimation of Christ, is one that may be fulfilled and complied with by ourselves as children of the Bridechamber, and that both the rejoicing and the mourning which He foretold, can go on in alternation even until He comes again. And if it can go on, I ask you to see in the text words even more constraining to that effect than a cold command that we rejoice over His birth and fast in view of His temptations, sufferings and death.

The whole forty days of Lent are thus days to us of sad and loving remembrance of a once suffering Saviour on earth. Forty days was the length of His fasting for our sakes. It is a strong suggestion of some voluntary denial of ours for His sake. We need the discipline for our own sake. But this is not now the point. Shall we fast for His sake? That is the question, and shall we not do it out of hearts of sympathy and gratitude for His sufferings? **If** we can answer this question in the affirmative, then all questions of the duty of fasting and abstaining from our own pleasures, relaxations and indulgences for six weeks, are abundantly answered to every loving follower of the Lord Jesus Christ. They are the six weeks of a Saviour's fasting for our sakes :—That is enough to be said.

Knowing that His sufferings ended in death at the last, what will you say and what will you do then with this commemorative season? Will you fall back on it as a mere season of the Church and satisfy yourselves with decent conformity to it, watching and fasting or not, as you think best?—or will you not look carefully into the will of your Lord concerning the children of the Bridechamber as signified by Him to His first disciples? The Church is here your schoolmaster to lead you to Christ, and if you cannot be helped by her ordinances and appointments to the better knowledge of Him, very little is the order of the Church worth to you. And if you cannot be helped to right feelings and right doings toward Him at this season, and be deeply impressed with the fitness of things as disclosed by the words of this text, then it seems to me that you can see no unfitness in going about your business or pleasure while mortal apprehension is waiting with all its distresses and alarms at your own doors. You can see no impropriety in going to the house of feasting at a time when your households are weeping, fasting and mourning. You might coldly ask in either case what good can my fasting or my intermission of business or pleasure do for my family or my circle of friends? How can it be of any service to them?—or why should I be turned away from my ordinary enjoyments till such time as the dying is dead and buried out of sight?

The answer to these questions rises at once to the lips of every right-hearted man and woman, and it is this,—that there is an everlasting fitness of things, and there are proprieties of life that cannot be violated without a shock to all concerned, and even to the outside world, though it has no special concern with the death, the suffering or the affliction that is going on. And is it not even so here, when Christ's death is to be contemplated and its proper commemoration prepared for? The sufferings that ended in it are brought constantly to mind, and the children of the Bridegroom are to contemplate Him as taken away from them, as He was taken from prison and from judgment and cut off out of the land of the living. The thought that He was wounded for our transgressions and bruised for our iniquities and that by His stripes we are healed, only exalts the fitness of things and the proprieties of life here well-nigh into moral necessities. The question is not why should we fast, but how can we help fasting and walking softly when the days come that the Bridegroom is taken away? He who knew what was in man knew what His loving, faithful disciples would do,—and so the prophecy of His own lips: "Then shall they fast in those days."

If any one can find room in his heart for the question:—How can He care, now that He is risen again from the dead, glorified and exalted at the right hand of God, that His children should be watching and fasting forty days with Him in His wilderness, and at His imaginary Cross, and waiting sadly at His empty sepulchre? —there is an answer to that question. Why did He care for that anointing of His body to the burying, at the hands of the woman with the alabaster box, when He knew that He should rise again the third day, the material body that she anointed changed into a spiritual and a glorious body? And yet we know that He did care, to the degree of making that loving deed a memorial of the woman who did it, as wide and as lasting as His gospel. And why again, in the Garden, when He had assured His disciples that they could not drink of His cup nor be baptized with His baptism, thus intimating the impossibility of their sharing His sufferings;— why did He pray them to tarry and watch with Him, and why did He ask them afterward by way of surprise or reproof,—" Could ye not watch with me one hour?" Why indeed, to all these questions, and to more that might easily be asked, but that He also was a man, and as keenly sensitive to all the decencies and proprieties of life as we are, and touched as we are by the sympathies of His friends.

And this same Jesus on His throne is no less alive to-day than He was here on earth to these things. Nay, He is Jesus Christ the same yesterday, to-day and forever. And because He is the same, there is the preciousness in Him which draws us toward Him as with cords of a man and bands of love.

Be assured, therefore, that He looks down upon His Church at this time, withdrawing into the wilderness with Him, as a bride putting on the weeds of her widowhood for the anniversary of His sufferings and death, ready to pass with Him in thought through the Valley of the Shadow of Death,—and that He asks of one of His children here and another there, who may be going their ways as at other times, —" Could ye not watch with me one hour?" and to the world outside that cares for none of these things, may He not well be supposed to say—" Is it nothing to you, all ye that pass by? Behold and see if there be any sorrow like unto my sorrow which is done unto me, wherewith the Lord hath afflicted me in the day of His fierce anger."

VIII.

HOW TO DO THE WILL OF GOD.

"Thy will be done."—St. Matt. vi. 10.

THIS petition of the Lord's prayer is many sided and comprehensive. Breathed without a mental reservation and out of a submissive spirit, it is as acceptable to God as prayer can be made, and reaches as high as the spirit of man can go toward its sanctity and perfection. It is blending the will of man with the will of God and making of both but one.

This may serve to show the value and importance of a life patterned upon the prayer of this petition. And it is to this rather than to the words, as prayer, that I would ask your attention on this occasion,—to a life, *i. e.*, whose governing principle and purpose is to do the will of God. I mean the will of God, not merely as that will is generally laid down for all of us in His word, but His special will as made known to each of us day by day, in the events that befall us and transpire around us, in the ever-shifting exigencies of life. These are the out-workings of God's will. They show what His will is for us who are affected by those workings, as we pass on through life.

And I would, on this occasion, illustrate what I mean by a Saviour's example. He declared that He came on earth, not to do His own will but the will of God and to finish His work. I need not say to any Christian, that it is safe to follow the steps of Christ's most holy life. He came on earth not only to do the will of God, but to leave us an example of the way to do it. In a book of two hundred pages called "A Day with Christ,"[1] the writer has selected one out of the few days of the Saviour's life on earth in which His steps may be quite clearly traced from morning until evening. The book was written to show how full of work His life was; how little was the rest or quiet He enjoyed, and how morally impossible it was, according to one of the Evangelists, to give a record of "all the things that Jesus did." The day chosen for this purpose is that on which St. Matthew was called to the apostleship.

This book gives the order of events on that day. It is with pains and probable accuracy that they have been arranged from the Gospel narrative. I give them here, not so much to show how busy was the day,—how much was

[1] Dr. Samuel Cox.

accomplished in it, or how incessant were the labors of Christ's life, but as an illustration of the way He did the will of God and wrought the petition of the text into His life, and so at last finished the work that had been given Him to do.

The day was spent in Capernaum,—His "home" as St. Mark calls it,—and through most of His active ministry it was His home. It was the day after His return from one of His journeys. Both the early morning and the night of that day were spent at home, so far as He could be said to have a home during those busy active years,—the last three of His life. And, therefore, the day may be taken as one of the ordinary days of the life set before us as an example for our own.

The first recorded event of the day was the assembling of a multitude of waiting friends, in the morning to greet Him. To this crowd He was speaking, when a man with the palsy was brought and had to be let down through the roof, uncovered for that purpose,—and so found his way to Jesus' feet. This incident put an end to His discourse to the multitude, and He proceeded to work upon the man before Him the miracle of healing. He wrought it in such a way as to necessitate a vindication of it, at some length, to the scribes and Pharisees present. This done, He went forth from the house to the seaside,—a short walk, where the multitude followed Him, and where He taught them. As He passed to the seaside, He saw Matthew sitting at the receipt of custom, and bade him follow. St. Matthew, leaving all, followed Him, with the multitude, to the seaside. The same day Matthew made Him a feast and invited the publicans and others, so that there was a great company at dinner. The inevitable scribes and Pharisees made their way to St. Matthew's house on the occasion, and began to find fault with Him to His disciples for eating with publicans. That brought from Him another vindication of Himself and a discourse on the subject of fasting. Then came another interruption to the feast. For while He spake these things, Jairus came to the house, and seeing Him, fell at His feet beseeching Him for his daughter. He rose from table, His disciples following, and started for the ruler's house. He was thronged again with the multitude as soon as He appeared in the streets. He was not allowed to reach the ruler's house uninterrupted.—The woman with the issue of blood came behind and touched Him. He paused long enough for a work of mercy in healing and converting the woman. While He was speaking to her, the news came that the ruler's daughter was dead; and as though the messenger had some pity for an overwrought man, he added "Why trouble the Master any further?" But Jesus hearing it, turned to the ruler and following on, said "Be not afraid, only believe." Arrived at the ruler's house amid the noise and confusion of the occasion, He wrought there His first recorded miracle of raising the dead. Even with this crowning work, the day's labors were not ended. The Saviour started for His home from the ruler's house and the night must have fallen as He did it. Relieved of the multitude, who had by this time either dispersed to their homes or were lingering about the ruler's house, giving vent to their astonishment, He failed to reach home uninterrupted. Two blind men followed Him into the house. Opening their eyes He dismissed them from His door with the words, "See that no one know it." And no sooner were these gone out than behold! there was brought to Him a dumb man, possessed of a devil. The devil was thereupon cast out and the dumb spake.

Now all this in one day, and possibly more than this. The morning began, with Christ at home, and back to that home in the evening we have now traced Him by all the steps we can find that He took. And we see in them His way of doing the will of God so that we may compare it with our own.

Now what I would call your special attention to here, and what you cannot help thinking of first of all, after the thought how busy was this day of Christ, is the fact that the things He did were one after another given Him to do in the simple order of Providence. One and all they were placed in His way, and so placed as to succeed each other in the most natural order. None was taken by Him out of that order,— none were left undone and there was no confusion, no doubt, hesitation or delay.

This history of a day, my brethren, sheds a flood of light upon those sayings of Christ's— "Sufficient unto the day is the evil thereof." "Take no thought for the morrow, for the morrow will take care of the things of itself"; "My meat is to do the will of Him that sent me and to finish His work," "Take my yoke upon you and learn of me for I am meek and lowly in heart." His yoke is here seen to be the having no will of His own, but a daily and hourly submission to the will of God. And His meekness and lowliness were shown in simply adopting the plan of His Father for the life He was to live. His study was to discern the will of God as to the method and order of His work and to follow it step, by step, as we follow a path opened for us by one who goes before us leading the way.

This is doing the will of God on earth as it is done in heaven. There the angels take their orders from the guiding of His eye and they watch and obey its every glance literally as servants of His that do His pleasure. And thus they act out the petition before us,—" Thy will be done as it is in heaven."

The question arises here, whether it is wrong to have what we call plans of life, and wrong to carry out those plans in the face of difficulties and interruptions, and whether in truth this is not the way to accomplish the most and do it the best. This is our danger and here we are liable to make our saddest mistakes;— mistakes which plunge us into mere endeavors to accomplish something and end in finishing nothing. For, constituted as we are, we must have some plan of life. Our mistake is that we have not the one thought uppermost of subordinating our plan at all times to the will of God. If made and carried out without this thought, it is our plan, not His, and it is more likely to diverge from than to coincide with the will of God. For what is the beginning of that divergence but self-will and trusting in self? And farther on self-conceit and self-glory. Or, on the other hand, if our plans fail, dissatisfaction with self,—impatience with our surroundings, —a murmuring and rebellious spirit toward God, and a sinking into the indifference or the helplessness of one who folds his hands and will do nothing;—or, worse, of one who persistently flies in the face of the Providence that attends his steps, yields to a temptation of the devil and is finally carried captive by him at his will.

Let me, before I close, point out some of the benefits,—I may say the blessedness, of following the steps of Christ's life on earth,—such as are here set before us.

First. Such a life is a constant means of grace,—a sanctifying life. It begins with the feeling of Hagar,—" Thou God seest me "—and it proceeds in lifting up the thoughts to Him as the eyes of a maiden to her mistress, in every change and chance of life, for an answer to the inquiry, "What will Thou have me to do?" We can but have wills and plans of our own, not for one day only but for many. With those wills and plans uppermost morning by morning for the days that pass, and with no regard for a possible contrary will working against them,—what shall we do with calls and occurrences such as beset the day of Christ outlined before us? We must needs regard and treat them as obstacles and interruptions to the work we have to do, and rid ourselves of them with all possible dispatch. If we do not ignore them altogether, we allow ourselves to be daily tried and provoked by them.

On the other hand let our plans be subordinated to the will of God, and we shall be looking for that will to be made known to us in just such calls as those to which our Lord and Saviour cheerfully yielded on that memorable day. And we shall take them as He did;—not as obstacles or interruptions, or as thwarting our plans of work, but as intimations of the different will and plan for us of God, and calling on us for the surrender or postponement of our wills implied in the words "Thy will not mine be done." And that is a sanctifying exercise. It has in it the essence of the holiness that God requires. Its results are a life of outward beauty and a life of inward strength. How gracefully and yet how strongly did He move from place to place on that busy day! He rested, as it were, from one good work by doing another, while on his way to a third, the greatest of all, and still using the time left him on his homeward walk to work the works of Him who sent Him, while it was day. Here was the Lord's prayer lived out through the day by Him who gave it, down to the ascription with which it closes,—" Thine is the Kingdom and the power and the glory."

Another side of the blessedness of following Christ's example of life, is that it is a life of peace to him who lives it. What is it that clouds our days with doubt,—marks their retrospect with weariness and discouragement and fills our nights with anxious thoughts for the morrow? It is, that because of obstacles and interruptions we accomplish so little. We have been delayed here and hindered there, so that the night comes to those who are wearied out and yet who seem to have done nothing,—nothing that was in their thoughts and plans to do. And so they are burdened with the feeling that they have lost a day,—lost a day here and a day there,—and they retire with the fear lest to-morrow shall be as this day, and they shall keep on forever toiling and taking nothing. It is a miserable and a wholly needless weariness and anxiety. Let the will of God, as shown by the workings of His providence, come into the busy days we live. Let it come how it will but only so that it cannot be mistaken, and then let us take it as His plan to the modifying or postponing of our own. We shall then take hold of obstacles and interruptions to our work with the conviction that these are God's next things for us to do, whatever may come after.

Let the possibility of these ever come into our preconceived plans or duties, and when they come let us take them as signs from God of what He would have us do. We shall begin and end our day's work in this way with the peace that they have who have cast their burden on the Lord, instead of struggling on under the yoke of our own unruly wills; and then, moreover, what we would do and what we are ever striving to do as a plan of life is to reach a certain desired goal, and it may be too hard for us. The different will of God may be discovered in the existence of some infirmity of nature,—or some drawback of circumstances. And then giving up that plan, and losing sight of that goal of our desires forever, is oftentimes the only way to peace of mind and to contentment with the lot assigned us. If He would that we should serve Him in some other and lower way, the will of God be done.

Finally:—A more blessed result still will come of doing the will of God after the example of Christ. In this way, and in this way only, can we finish our work. What a triumphant exclamation was that on the cross, when gathering up out of the word of God the last item of prophecy unfulfilled, and drinking the last dregs of a bitter cup, He could say as He did,—"It is finished." Why could He with truth say it, but that from day to day through life, and that nothing be lost, He was engaged in gathering the intimations of His Father's will from the Book of His written word, and that of His daily providence, and making the doing of that the condition of His life.

Let us compare a life complete and rounded like this, with lives such as we see and hear of from day to day, if we are not ourselves living them. Here is one cut down, as we are prone to say,—untimely—a premature death. His work is not done,—hardly begun,—no plan of His life completed, and no hope realized. All His dreams and aspirations have come down to a heap of ashes. Shall we who have just begun to live and labor, and we who have got farther along,—whether in the morning or in the midday of our plans and dreams of life,— shall we go on parting ever with precious time that can never return and letting it go with a pang of regret that we missed the things we might have done, and the things we ought to have done, till the night comes when no man can work? Let not a broken column stand over our graves to tell of unfinished work or an unfinished life. Let us stop prying and peering into the future or longing and laboring for that which may never be ours. Let us rather look up day by day to Him who will show us step by step the way we are to take. The night may then close around us when it will, and darkness even unto death come upon us. It will neither find us unprepared, nor the work unfinished that God has given us to do.

IX.

LIMITS OF THE DIVINE PATIENCE.

"For I say unto you that none of those men that were bidden shall taste of my supper."—St. Luke xiv. 24.

It is hard to convince men of sin from their non-compliance with the appointments of Christ's religion. If they choose to treat them with indifference for reasons in which they see no sin or crime, whose concern they say is it but our own? If we are losers by such a course, the loss is ours. No one else is harmed or need be troubled. Making a sin out of what has no criminality or immorality about it, is an undeserved reflection upon people of fair characters. It is condemning them for their opinions; and that is bigotry and intolerance.

I have here described a very common state of mind, brought about by the urgency with which the invitations of the Gospel are pressed upon people not ready to yield to them. They will not admit that their conduct needs defence or excuse. Should they make answer to the demand made upon them, and to the reasons and arguments by which it is enforced, the answer would be very short and decisive. Go your ways and we will go ours. We respect your religious posture. Pay the same respect to ours. If you see sin and wrong in our attitude toward the religion which you preach or which you practise, you see what we do not and will not admit. We may be wrongdoers but not in this. And if you are wrongdoers, your religion will not help you.

I wish I could adequately set forth, to those who see no sin and no wrong in this attitude, the claims of the gospel as shadowed forth in the parable of the great supper from which the text is taken. For there are sins and wrongs which have never yet been defined by law. They are not forbidden in so many words in the decalogue, and human laws take little notice of them. But there are sins and wrongs of a man against his brother and against his Maker, other than those upon which we can lay the hands of the law. There are deeper sins and graver offences than law or language can easily define, which lie under the letter.

For example: There are the kindly instincts of a common humanity, and these instincts are laws that define for every one of us what is sin and what is wrong. St. Paul speaks of a law written on "fleshly tables." And it is as constraining as a written "thus saith the Lord," or thus saith the law of justice, honesty or morality. There are laws of propriety that have their origin and their sanction in the fitness of things. The swift condemnation of man passes against his fellow man upon every violation of them; and that judgment is as universal as the condemnation that passes upon his falsehood or dishonesty. It places him outside the social pale, and oftentimes more suddenly and effectually than do his sins and crimes.

Rare are the men and women, who will violate the usages of respectable social intercourse. They would as soon violate the laws of the land. We are social as well as moral beings, and the most of us are as scrupulous concerning the social as the moral that is in us. The people we have in mind would, commonly, sooner violate the moral than the social instincts of their natures.

And it is a great mistake to suppose that God, who gave us both sets of instincts, is content with appealing to only one of them in His own behalf. He appeals to both.

In this parable of the great supper, He puts the conduct of the neglecters of His Gospel in the light of setting at naught the reciprocities of social intercourse. He makes the gospel here not merely a gift, as they who neglect it understand it to be, but just such a gift on both sides as a feast with its invitations and its preparations. And this is the side that its neglecters will not look at nor regard. To them it has only one side, and that is, an offer to them of what, if they do not see its virtue or feel the need of it, they may give it the go-by as a thing of course, and as the end of a very simple matter. Far enough is this from being the end of it. The most affecting aspect of the Gospel is thus missed altogether. And that is the solicitude and the good-will toward themselves of the Divine Giver.

They do not consider this. They do not think of the effect of their indifference and their neglect upon Him who offers the gift. And it is their want of thought and consideration here that constitutes the sin and the wrong of their neglects. They are bound to consider it. How would it sound in the ears of the offerer of a feast, to hear from his invited guests such an answer as this: "We beg to be excused," and that without any allusion whatever to the cost and trouble to which the offerer of the feast has been put on their account. It does not occur to them, that they owe anything to his care or consideration for them, nor why their neglect should be followed by his disappointment, and least of all by the sting as of an insult in view of their excuses. Such a reply as this even in thought would prove, yourselves being judges, your utter unworthiness of his respectful attention. It would be adding, as we say, insult to injury. It would prove beyond all dispute that kindness has not only been thrown away on unwilling, but unworthy objects; that it has not waked up the first thought and the most affecting about it, namely, the generous and disinterested intent of it, the cost and pains attending it, and the contempt that its neglect puts upon the working of the tenderest and most precious sympathies of our common nature.

Yes, my dear friends, it is here, where the mass of its neglecters never think of looking for it, that the awakening and moving power of our religion is found. You who neglect it have concluded that you can get along without it, and so you let it go for things that you think more to your present advantage.

Now just that is the way the invitations of the parable were treated. The invited guests thought they could do better than to accept it; and so they went off to their business or their pleasure without a thought of what the feast was costing their friend, and without thinking of the effect of their excuses upon him.

And this proves that they never felt the power nor the constraint of the invitation. No tenderness of feeling grew out of it; no gratitude to the giver, no appreciation of his sacrifices for their sakes.

Even so it is with the mass of those who neglect the great salvation. By nature, and by habit even more, we have little relish for what it offers. We cannot, except poorly and inadequately, appreciate what it will do for us. There are other things that promise better. There are enjoyments and engagements with which it seems to conflict. And so we let it go, and it must be confessed that we do it very easily, our feelings and affections not having been enlisted and our preferences being already fixed elsewhere.

I am glad to believe, however, that there are those here whom I address every Lord's day, who would be glad to appreciate the offered salvation at its worth. Not personally or wholly committed to it, they would yet be glad to have their love and gratitude laid hold of by this gospel. And there are others lamenting the fact that they have not the relish they ought to have nor the interest they ought to feel for the duties and privileges of their religion. I would speak to-day a word to such. And that word is this.

Leave off your way of looking at the claims of Christ's religion. Stop weighing and balancing its pleasures against those of the world, in the course of which you will find yourselves choosing the world and rejecting Christ. And look at His religion on its other side. Look at the good-will that is in it toward yourselves. Consider what it cost Him to offer it, rather than what you have thought it worth to yourselves.

This is the way that right-hearted people come to valuing and accepting the offers of some good by their fellow men. They reason that what cost a thoughtful giver much, must be worth something to the receiver, and that it is at least worth their trying. They will say to themselves, it is due to our kind and thoughtful neighbor that we should taste of his hospitality; due to him that we should consider what his kindness toward us has cost him, and that we cannot do otherwise and preserve his respect. If he has been at the cost of serious sacrifices on our behalf, it may be that what he offers is too precious to be rejected, and that rejection of it may be our irretrievable loss. Such an attitude as this toward God, the attitude natural, almost inevitable toward a fellow man, will bring you face to face with that great Being as His Gospel was designed to bring you. You will consider His mind and will with regard to you, where heretofore you have consulted only your own interest or pleasure. In this way you will come to the conclusion that the salvation of the Gospel is a more serious thing than you thought. Finding that it cost the Giver His life you will conclude it worth to you more than you can easily comprehend. You will try perhaps, and try in vain to account for the shameful death of Christ in some way that has not laid you under a lasting obligation to Him. You will find its secret in this: that "God so loved the world." And you will begin to be amazed and ashamed of your reasons and your excuses for neglecting it.

You have loosely thought that God is not a man that He should care for the treatment accorded to this Gospel by one of His creatures. But you will find that He does care, by the strongest of all proofs that He spared not His own Son for your sakes. And you will know it too from this very parable in which He likens Himself to one of you as the Giver of a feast. You will stop dreaming of impunity at the last, and have the truth born in upon you that here is a God whose patience may be exhausted, and whose love and solicitude must turn, at some point, into an assertion of Himself against the rejecters and despisers of His mercy, and declare at last that none of those men that were bidden shall taste of His supper.

108 *LIMITS OF THE DIVINE PATIENCE.*

Learn from all this my brethren, that a life of outward conformity to the rule of right and wrong, and one of indifference to the ordinances and behests of a distinctive Christianity is far enough from what either propriety or duty requires. Such a life is no tolerable return to the God who made us with instincts that tell us what return we ought to make. It avails little with our fellow men, that we refrain from violence, fraud or crime against their persons or estates; though there be men who take to themselves no little credit even for this. There is something due to them beyond this, and if it be withheld and neglected, they feel the wrong more keenly than they feel the effect of bodily harm. They have feelings to be respected. They have a sense of personal dignity and self-respect. And so we all have, and we must lose our manliness and womanliness when we cease to respect these things in one another. The last offence we will commit in cold blood is to rob a neighbor here. But will a man who refrains from robbing a neighbor, rob God? If we turn a deaf ear to His pleading voice in the Gospel and persist in it, what but robbery can He call such treatment as that?

You keep the last six commandments of His decalogue. Why do you do it? Not so much because you respect Him, as because you have some regard for your neighbors and your characters.

What do you do to show your respect for God your Maker? You may think you are doing many things; but I ask you who neglect the gospel what will they avail when He has made your respect for this gospel and your acceptance of it the test of your regard for His will?

If the Gospel of Christ is the truth of God and not a mere human device, then whatever else God has done for us and however we have treated Him in return for it, here at last stands His Son. If another parable conveys to us the truth, He has said: "They will reverence my Son." In other words: "I will try them with one last touching display of my mercy and love toward them; and if they resist this, then I give them up. They will receive my well-beloved Son, or they are no longer worthy of the mercy I offer."

And thus it is that men and women are tested in the sight of God. Refusal here must surely be answered for at the last day.

And now shall He apply that test to any soul here, or shall He continue to test it to the end in vain? Shall such an invitation as this of the Almighty to his creatures, fall on a single ear without stirring the soul and all that is within it? Shall it fail to awaken the sense that God has implanted in us of the everlasting fitness of things? Dare any one reply with the excuse or apology for not complying with it, that there are hindrances to the honor due from him to God? that he is hindered by care; hindered by business; hindered by pleasure? The naming of these hindrances over, yourselves being judges, is a confession of your unworthiness, and if persisted in " Of how sore a punishment, suppose ye, shall he be thought worthy, who hath trodden under foot the Son of God?"

One thought in conclusion and it is this: When a man acts out the honorable instincts that are in him toward his Maker as toward his neighbor, he has little more to do in order to be a Christian. He is one already in all but the name. To such a man I have only to say, "Arise and be baptized and wash away thy sins;" or, come with a true penitent heart and a lively faith and be reckoned among the welcome guests at the table of the Lord.

X.

PEACE IN BELIEVING.

"Now the God of hope fill you with all joy and peace in believing."—Romans xv. 13.

THESE three words sum up the richest earthly blessing of the Gospel, as do those other words of the apostle that, "we which believe do enter into rest." This peace or rest is a state of the mind and also of the affections. It may consist with much external disturbance. It comes often at no little cost, and it is sometimes long in coming. There is a great deal of ordinary believing where peace does not come; and it may be true and sincere believing, only it does not go far enough or deep enough. And so to such this scripture is a promise to the ear that is broken to the hope.

I will venture on this occasion to touch upon this part of Christian experience. Let me begin by saying that I do not doubt either the sincerity or the intelligence of a believer, who says that he fails of peace in his believing. He may believe in all the Christian verities, not doubting of a single article of the saving faith of the Gospel and yet fail of peace. What do I say to this? I say, in the first place, that he does not go far enough with his believing. Believing, in the religious sense of the word, means not merely accepting a truth as such, and that sincerely; but it means appropriating that truth to the lack and the want in one's self that it was designed to supply. This appropriation is an unseen process, but it answers to the outward one of taking and eating food by a hungry man. He believes, not merely that it is satisfying food, which he might do to the end and never find the satisfaction he believed in, but go hungering all the while. He must believe to the point of taking the food. So with the truth of the Gospel and belief in it.

Believing in its atonement for sin and its forgiveness is no mere act or assent of the intellect. That is feeding on wind. My believing in the atonement is believing that it has reached my sins and blotted them out of the book of God's remembrance. That blots them out of mine, and thus I have peace in believing. I admit that this act of faith is a higher and a harder thing to reach than merely to credit a truth. But a truth fully and beyond all doubt taken into the head, will tend to sink by its own worth and weight to the heart where its virtue is felt more or less to casting out fear. The doubt that still may stand in the way of peace is whether the conditions of God's forgiveness have been complied with on our part, and that is, whether our repentance is sincere and whether, after all, it is accepted. A doubt here will keep peace out of the mind as effectually as a lack of faith in the word of God.

Here let me say then, that there are easily applied outward tests for a truly repenting and believing man. He is not called to grope his way uncertainly among the feelings, experiences and inward workings of his mind. His past life lies open to his inspection and his recollection. His sins to be repented of are there. His memory and his conscience will bring him face to face with them, as they stand in the light of God's own countenance. And then whether his mind is made up to forsake them he knows, and whether he has set about the work he knows; and he knows moreover, or may know, that a resolute and sincere beginning to live a new life, relying on the Grace of God, is all that is required for his sins past; and whether this beginning of a new life is accepted of God he may also know, by divinely appointed tokens of assurance when he comes forward with the public confession and steadfast purpose which God requires.

That assurance is a personal one to the man

and comes to him from God in the shape of signs and pledges visible, tangible and ordained for that purpose. The sacraments of the Church are divinely appointed to this end. In them is contained the pledge and promise of God's forgiveness. In them we may truly say is His word confirmed with an oath that by "two immutable things in which it was impossible for God to lie, we might have strong consolation," or in the words of the text, "peace in believing."

We know what an anxious sinner needs by what he says and does at turning points in his religious life. I believe, he says, that Christ died for my sins and I repent of them. God is witness to my sincerity. Well then, I ask, what more do you want? I want, he says, assurance, some demonstration from above, or some sensible impression on my spirit, which will make sure to me the promise on God's side, to accept my repentance and to forgive my sins. We have perhaps all known, if we have not ourselves experienced, feelings and frames of mind which are trusted in, or distrusted, according as they are hopeful on the one hand or despondent on the other. The subject of them has often cried peace to himself, when there is no peace that lasts; or, he vacillates between hope and fear till he knows not what to believe or what to do. He wants assurance from God. He wants, what a preacher who made light of the sacraments of the Gospel once called, "an authoritative or finishing touch from heaven" before he can have peace. It is an instinctive want, and this preacher recognized it as such while yet he made light of it, for he failed to point out the ground of any such assurance in the Gospel. But in the command to the sinner to arise and be baptized and wash away his sins, we see where and what this authoritative touch from heaven is. And the same authoritative touch is disclosed in the other sacrament as this Church has received it, when we heartily thank the ever-living God that He "assures us thereby of His favor and goodness toward us, and that we are very members incorporate in the mystical body of His Son, and are also heirs through hope of His everlasting kingdom."

Here then is, "the peace in believing" which is promised in the text. But we must go a little farther. Peace is so fluttering and timid a guest from heaven, that though in the breast it is ever ready to take wing and be gone at the first returning occasion for distrust or alarm. Temptation alone cannot disturb this peace of God, and we ought to remember this. Temptation resisted serves only to fortify the peace within and anchor it more firmly there. If this peace of mind and conscience be disturbed, it is because temptation is yielded to. We may always know when that happens, and then there is nothing but to rise from a fall and do the first works over again, to reopen the soul to the old and precious truth that Christ died for our sins, claim our share in his atonement and believe, even to seeking anew, the ordained tokens of pardon and acceptance with God. Nothing is impossible to him that believeth, and so we ever go on to find,

> "New perils past, new sins forgiven,
> New thoughts of God, new hopes of heaven."

But again, as already intimated, there is peace of soul as well as peace of mind and conscience to be had in believing; and here again believing is prone to stop short with us of little faith. Our peace is disturbed by fears and anxieties for our earthly future, and that of those dear to or dependent upon us; by regrets and hankerings that go back to the past; and by the annoyances and irritations of the present. Thus past, present and future come before us one after another, and sometimes all combine to disturb our peace. If peace can follow believing in all these ways, there is no other way in which our hearts can be disturbed. There are those then whose discontent and uneasiness come out of their memories. They seem to themselves when they think of it,—and they are constantly recurring to the past,—that they have floated away from the innocence, the happiness or the usefulness of other and better days. They compare the present with the former days to the continual disparagement of themselves, and to the disturbance of their peace. In this they are often mistaken or deceived. What an intolerable bondage that was of the Jews to the Egyptians! As we read its actual history, it was lighted with scarcely a ray of comfort or of hope. And yet, when the yoke was broken from their necks, we find them at the first step forward toward a land of freedom, hankering after what they called "the flesh pots of Egypt," where they said and doubtless thought, they did eat bread to the full. Their memories had deceived them. They looked on the dark side of the present and made it the background on which they painted their fancy picture of the past.

There is scarcely a man or woman here who would fain go back and live what they call their better days, who is not deluded in the same way. It is one of the mercies of God that the evils, the trials and the bitter things of the past fade into gradual indistinctness, while the pleasant recollections survive. The death of friends, were it not for this mercy, would make a daily funeral march of the whole subsequent life. And so with other trials we have passed through. The edge of them is dulled and worn off by the lapse of time. The past thus comes before us as one of the solaces of life. We may trace the hand of a merciful and loving God in this. But that same mercy is over and around us still. And faith in that, and believing it, brings peace to a longing, restless heart. The God who thus comes out of the past as a God of goodness and mercy, has neither left nor forsaken us in the present, and we need not go backward to find Him. He is about our steps to-day enabling us to lay up a store of better recollections for the days to come.

Therefore, roam no longer restless or hankering over the irrecoverable past, when you may go forward with the words of the Psalmist sounding in your ears, "Surely goodness and mercy shall follow me all the days of my life and I will dwell in the house of the Lord forever."

Then once more, there is the future, out of which is apt to come, even more than out of the past, that which is disturbing our peace. The young sometimes look forward with an impatience that forbids all present content. And the older and more thoughtful incline to people the future with evil, sickness, calamity, poverty disgrace, death. Shall we say they do not believe in God? The shocks of evil and the bolts of death, and the creeping, steady approach of life's sorrowful changes, derive their power to disturb our peace from the fear that they may come suddenly—that they will find us unprepared—that they will come in their worst shapes—that they will come without their compensations and perhaps, worst of all, that they will come all together to our utter distraction. Apprehensions like these must be met by an exercise of faith, easier far to reach, than to travel on in fear and uncertainty. Who then, but a God of mercy, stands in the unknown future of our lives, with the dreaded seeds in His hands, of all the sorrowful things that can happen to us? Yes; who but He?

And He has said to every one of us, " As thy days so shall thy strength be." Believing in God is believing what He says. It is believing in what He will do, from what He has already done. What is it that the anxious, fearful soul would have in the death, the suffering, the sorrow that must come? He would have strength to bear it, he would have wisdom to turn it to good account, and the ability to bring good out of it. Give him this and you give him an antidote to fear. You open to him the way to peace. The future will be turning its brighter side to such a believer day by day. With the trials will come their uses and their compensations.

And so it is, my dear brethren, that what we are to do to have peace in view of the future, is just to send our believing forward as far as our fears and anxieties go. The near and dark horizon will thus be moved for us farther and farther away, and the perspective down to the end of life will be brightened by a lively faith in the comforting and strengthening presence of the God of peace.

I have no time, on the present occasion, to speak of the peace which may take the place of the daily irritations and provocations of life. They flee before the first determined upward look in the faith that, "thou God seest me." All wrath, anger, clamor and discontent will fade away before the glance of that all-seeing eye. Peace will come to a troubled soul, such as He spake on earth to the winds and the waves.

Finally, let us remember that peace in believing is a goal that must be reached, if there be the growth in grace that proves the Christian to be alive unto God.

We must go on from believing to peace of mind, and peace of soul, ere the Holy Spirit of God, always fluttering and never settling upon turbid waters, can enter in and dwell there, and finish His work of sanctifying body, soul and spirit, to a meetness for the inheritance of the saints in light.

XI.

THE SIN OF THE PRODIGAL SON.

"And the younger of them said to his father, father give me the portion of goods that falleth to me."—St. Luke xv. 12.

BY common consent the Parable of the Prodigal Son, more than any other, has in it the pith and marrow of the gospel. It has been called the gospel within the gospel, so clearly stand forth in it the great features of man's fall and recovery.

If we can take a Scripture story, shadowed forth in real life so often as to become everyday and familiar history, as a fair illustration of Spiritual truths, it would seem that our religion ought to be divested of much of the mystery with which it comes laden to many, and be plain and level to the commonest understanding, so that no one need doubt of its conditions or its requirements upon him. In the hope that this may prove to be the case with those before me, I ask your attention to the Parable of the Prodigal Son.

THE SIN OF THE PRODIGAL SON. 123

The father brought before us here had two sons. One, the elder, may be called the obedient son, in distinguishing him from his younger brother. And yet his obedience evidently had not the source and spring it ought to have had. It was a formal rather than a filial obedience. And his conduct in the end serves as a background for the better showing forth of the glad and willing return of the prodigal to his home and his filial allegiance. As such a foil therefore we may regard the elder son, so far as the present purpose is concerned.

There are other lessons to be drawn from his character and conduct, even as there are many sides to the parable. Here let us take the one of the younger son that shows us plainly first, what sin is at its root and in its virus, and then secondly, what at its root repentance is.

We hear much in our day, and vague talk it largely is, respecting the Fatherhood of God. Let us learn from this Scripture, what it really is, and what is Sonship in man, and what are their power and virtue in the work of our salvation.

First then : There was no suddenness in the thought of the prodigal that led him to ask for the portion of goods that was to fall to him. There was no abruptness in this demand, such as may strike us on the surface of the story. We know indeed that such a demand as this of an earthly son upon his father must have a history behind it. And it is a history of inward restlessness, and a growing longing to be rid of home ties and trammels and of a condition of filial dependence.

With that portion of goods to which he had accustomed himself to look forward as his own to do what he would with it, he could take care of himself, free from all further filial subordination and service, and be his own master.

The longer such a thought was in his mind the stronger it grew there, till the final break came in the demand of the text:—Give me my portion and let me go. That thought weaker or stronger, is beating in youthful bosoms to-day all around us. It is restrained from breaking out by an inborn repugnance to severing the tie that binds the son to his father. For it is a tie of nature, one of the deepest and the most binding as it is among the most worthy that belongs to us. And the Father must let it go. What else could he do? If the prodigal had staid on after such a demand was refused to him, his inward estrangement would only have increased, and the tie of fatherhood grown more and more intolerable. The love of a father leads him to comply with the demand in the hope and prayer for a son's repentance and better mind.

Need we go any farther in order to show what the sin was of the prodigal son. He gathered all together, his own indeed it now was, and took his departure into a far country. But with the inward link broken that bound him to his father, the real departure had already been taken. The heart had gone into a far country and it was little that body and goods should follow hard upon it. Then come the wasting, and the rioting till the portion of goods is gone, and the mighty famine follows, and the prodigal comes to want. It may loosely be said, that here was the sin—the sin of wasting that gives its name to the parable, and the sin of riotous living. And sins indeed they are. But here they are the fruits of his root sin, even as the beggary and want that followed them. All are leaves and branches of a tree whose poison is to be found in its root. And that root is the loosening and the severing of the tie of sonship. To change the figure, here was the fountain of all the bitter waters that this young man went on to drink. And it was a fountain opened by his own deliberate choice. No doubt it cost him something. He had to stifle more or less of natural affection in order to make it. He had to forget or ignore years of loving parental care and vigilance and protection in a father's house, where all that the father had was his. And so the prodigal himself regarded it when he came to himself.

And now let us pass from the prodigal's sin to his repentance. What was that? What was it that he felt to his sorrow and his regret? The first sign he gave of any softened feeling, was a tender thought of the father and the home he had left. This led him on to a longing for a place, even the condition of servitude in that house, now that he had broken the closer tie that once bound him to it. And so he says " I will arise and go to my father " and confess my sin. It was no sin or crime of his recent life, not the wasting, nor the rioting, nor the prodigality, of which he was thinking first or foremost. But it was the sin of ignoring and severing the tie that binds a son to his father. It was the sin of an ungrateful casting off of a father's care, and the resolve to be his own master. And so he says I will do my best to repair the breach I have committed, by putting myself once more under my father, and if he will no longer own me I will yet own him and serve him. And so he arose and went and did as he resolved. We may ask was this his repentance for his sin, and the whole of it? In answer I can say, no other or further repentance is named. I can say more—that this prodigal's repentance and reparation are just the repentance and reparation that go to an earthly father's heart, for a course of filial unworthiness, even as the prodigal shows us. The result ever has been and ever will be complete and perfect reconciliation, where natural affection survives or revives between a father and a son.

And now to apply this truth to the case of a sinner against God. What is the root sin to be confessed and repented of before Him, so that the indispensable conditions of our religion, repentance and faith may be complied with? Is it to be found in a sinful course of life, excesses, rioting, drunkenness, debauchery, recklessness of conduct, evil example, lawlessness, wastefulness, or prodigality? Here, indeed, are sins, and it may be crimes to be repented of. And many a man sets about the work of repairing his shattered condition, health and reputation, and carrying on the work to the point of regaining, perhaps, all that he has lost. But is this the repentance toward God that religion requires, or is it repentance for his sin? The answer is that however becoming it may be, it does not touch the root of the poisonous tree—though God forbid that any man should be checked or restrained in it by word or sign. Let him, therefore, go on hacking off of his life every evil habit, and stripping his character and his example of every hateful excrescence. At the same time let him understand that there is a root sin, even as there is a root faith without which it is impossible to please God. That sin is severing or ignoring the filial relationship between him and his God. The great, the crowning fact of man on earth is his sonship in God.

And then, secondly, the faith which religion requires, what is that? The apostle speaks of it as a faith that works by love, and purifies the heart. In view of all that is said about it in Scripture and in the parable before us, which had better be called the parable of the forgiving and rejoicing father, than that of the prodigal son, men, even distinguished writers of critical books on religion, will have it that a moral life is to all intents and purposes a religious life, and that the ethics, as they call it, of the gospel constitute all that is of worth in the religion of the gospel. "Conduct," declares one of these men, "is three-fourths of life," and he declares it as though good conduct needed no deeper root or spring than that of a decent self-respect, and a moderate regard for the welfare of the community.

I have rejoiced to get hold of a wiser and a

better book,[1] written in order to meet and correct some of the mistakes of modern skepticism. In his synopsis of the first chapter or essay in this book the author defines faith even as the parable shadows it forth. He declares faith to be the "motion in man of his sonship in the Father. It is the conscious recognition and realization of our inherent filial relationship to God." In this motion or instinct was the returning faith, and thereupon followed the repentance of the prodigal son. And I need hardly say it was the spring in him, as it is the spring in every truly repenting sinner, of his new and better life. It is the basis of a full and mutual reconciliation between a sinner and his God.

Bearing in mind that man was made in the image of God, and that our Elder Brother came on earth to mirror forth that image in its distinctness, what will you or can you say now of the mirror which this parable of Christ's own speaking exhibits? Can there be a doubt as to what He regards as the sin of man against his Maker, and what in the son are the faith and repentance He looks for? Every father and every son among us, who feels the tie that binds them together must know what it is, and therefore what both sin and repentance **must**

[1] Lux Mundi.

be. What was the father in the parable looking for and what was he waiting for? For what was he solicitous, and for what finally were the feasting and the rejoicing? It was not over the outward reformation of a grievous offender against good morals, or good order. It was not over the recovery to decency of life of a man sunk in the mire of sensuality—all this indeed by the way and as a consequence of something deeper down, more precious and more abiding. It was over a son whose sonship had died within him, but was alive again, and over a tie of kindred that had been lost and was found. Put it to yourselves, ye fathers, shadowing forth toward your children as ye do the mind of God toward us all, and tell me, if the hearing by the father in the parable of his son's reformation in that far country, of his respectability and his prosperity there, would have sufficed to wipe out the sin and the shame of that son in his father's estimation, or gone an inch toward repairing the wrong he had done? You know it would not. Know then by this token the meaning of the words, "repent ye and believe the gospel."

Let me close with some words to those who yet have the first works of their religion to do, and with a word to those who are striving to live answerably to their heavenly calling.

THE SIN OF THE PRODIGAL SON. 131

The great stumbling-block in the way of a conscious sinner's repentance such as the prodigal son's, exists chiefly in his imagination. He has been living the time past of his life away from God, and possibly indulging in excesses or dishonesties. There is a feeling of shame, and there ought to be in all this, and God forbid that I should make light of it! But I say to every such man, whatever have been the sins or crimes of his life against God or man, that they need not and ought not to stand one hour in the way of his return to the God who made him, or the Saviour who came on earth to disclose the love toward man of His Father and ours. You cannot remove these sins if you would. And the blessed truth remains in spite of them, that you have to do with a God who is waiting to be gracious, and who may be said to long for the renewing and rebinding of the severed tie between a father and a son. Repentance, my dear friends, why your simple response in heart and will to the fact of a Father in heaven is repentance. It is repentance at the root of the tree, and its virtue runs like a shock of electricity up through the trunk and out through the branches of a bad character and an evil life. It follows then that the faith required is but the realization of the fact of a returning son and a rejoicing father. It is believing that the spark which has begun to glow in a filial bosom kindles afresh the love of a Father who is in Heaven. And, so I say, if the sincere confession be yours that you are unworthy to be called His sons, and yet you crave the knitting again of the tie of sonship, be assured again and again that it suffices for Him that His son was dead and is alive again, that he was lost and is found.

To those who have so far responded to the love of God as to have remained in their Father's house, I have this word to say. Take heed and beware of self-righteousness, envy or uncharitableness. These were the sins of the elder brother, and you hear them breaking out of his own mouth in the words: "Lo! these many years do I serve thee, and yet thou never gavest me anything." Let not our service degenerate into a cold, calculating idea of equivalent, so much service for so much remuneration. The tie of sonship may be worn in this way to the thinnest attenuation and that of brotherhood broken in twain, as it was broken here by the brother of the prodigal.

Finally, let us all enter into the nobler liberty of sons of God. "For we have not received the spirit of bondage again to fear, but we have received the Spirit of adoption whereby we cry Abba, Father."

"The Spirit itself beareth witness with our spirits that we are children of God, and if children then heirs, heirs of God and joint heirs with Christ, the elder brother of us all."

XII.

THE TEST OF CHRISTIAN DISCIPLESHIP.

"Now if any man have not the Spirit of Christ, he is none of His."—Romans viii. 9.

The Spirit of Christ I think must here be taken to mean not distinctly the Holy Ghost, but the mind of Christ; the temper and disposition that were in Him. There is such a thing as the Christlike mind, and the apostle in the text seems to mean that one who lacks this is not Christ's, does not, so to speak, belong to Him. He certainly speaks here of something a Christian must have, if he is indeed such, whatever else he lacks. There are defects and demerits that may be made up to him. Some virtue may be imputed to him for Christ's sake, and he may be treated as though it were his own, but not this. The spirit and temper of Christ we must have, in order to be sharers in the virtue, of His death. Without this He must say to us at the last "I never knew you."

We seem, my dear brethren, to have come here upon a crucial test of our holy religion;

upon the edge of that sword of the spirit which is the word of God, discerning the thoughts and intents of the heart. There is applied to us here a solemn and heart-searching test of our Christian character.

Let us humbly inquire in the first place what in particular was this spirit of Christ, the one deep principle in Him here referred to; and afterward apply to ourselves some of the tests by which we may know, each one of us for ourselves, whether or not we have that spirit.

First then, we may be sure that a life of such unity and completeness as His had some undeviating, controlling and discoverable rule or principle at the bottom of it, and that it sufficed to carry Him through all his labors and support him through all His temptations to the end. I would not characterize the Spirit of Christ in this unhesitating way, if there were really a doubt about it, or if any mixed or complicated motive could be attributed to Him. The Scripture has left us in no doubt here and in no liability to mistake. The mind of Christ is not hidden from us. It was declared before He came into the world, and found utterance when He came, at His own lips, and it went on to be illustrated throughout His life. To know what it was, I call your attention to the fortieth Psalm, which is expressly applied to

Him, in the tenth Chapter to the Hebrews where He is represented as speaking thus: "In the volume of the Book it is written of me, Lo I come to do Thy will O my God. Yea, Thy law is within my heart." This lets us know with what mind He came into the world, and that it was a mind made up of entire obedience and submission to the will of God. In order that He might show forth this mind, and manifest to the world the spirit that was in Him, God prepared Him a body. "A body hast thou prepared me." Thus the mind of Christ was foreshadowed before He came. After He came, His own lips told forth the errand that brought Him here and told it with an emphasis. "I came not to do my own will but the will of Him that sent me" and, "my meat is to do the will of Him that sent me and to finish His work."

These solemn utterances cover the entire ground of Christ's human life and explain it. This discovery of the spirit that was in Him throws light upon His past eternity. It accounts for His Incarnation. It illumines all the way He took through life even to the hour of His death. It accounts for His life and His death; "not my will but thine be done." With His last words, "It is finished," the will of God for Him was completed and done. This then was the spirit of Christ and the mind that was in Him. And you will agree with me that no spirit, purpose, or principle of a human being, was ever carried out and carried through to its perfection and its fulfilment in the face of so many difficulties; through so much suffering, or at such a fearful cost as this of our Redeemer. Not that we are bound to leave behind us such tokens of the Christlike spirit as were afforded by Him who suffered for us, in the doing of His Father's will. Our doings and endurings must needs fall short of His; such extremes as these are not expected of us. He who suffered for us remembereth that we are dust, and how hard it is for us to do the will of God or even to say " Thy will be done."

We are indeed held to a stricter doing and enduring of the will of God than many of us seem to imagine. But it is not the strictness of our doings that is here made the test. If it were, who indeed would stand? It is not the perfection of our doings to which we are bound as the condition of our being Christ's. But the underlying, animating principle of His life must be the animating principle of ours. The spirit must be willing, though the flesh be weak. And that will send us through life toward the end which our Saviour reached; and it will hold our wills that way, even as the needle after every trembling variation, settles ever toward the pole. And therefore do I say, that so far as we are required to be like Christ, on pain of being disowned by Him, we can be like Him. It is no impossible thing for any human being to take the will of God for the law of his life and carry it with him to the day of his death.

But let me define what I take to be the spirit of Christ so as to bring it down to the level of every man's thorough understanding as the spring and motive of his own life. It is to be distinguished from other not unworthy motives and principles of human conduct. I call the mind of Christ in us then, *a sense of duty*, as distinguished from those impulses of our nature, our love and affection, our hope or fear. Not that the latter are unworthy motives. There is a basis for them all in the human constitution. The religion of Christ includes them all and takes man as he is, calling forth all the good that is in him. It has its motives and persuasives to address to all the faculties and susceptibilities that God has given us. But it lays hold of this one, the sense of duty, which is in every man, and exalts it above the rest.

Who cannot act from a sense of duty, be he heathen or Christian? Impulses toward God and goodness may vary; they may be weak in some men and wanting in others; they may vary from day to day in the same breast. Hope and fear may be weak from mere dulness of imagination. The glow of all these forces of our nature may be feeble and flickering without our fault, and they are hard to be discovered in desponding minds.

And so the great test is not high wrought feeling, not the force of hope or fear, nor any other impossibility. It is an humbler, a broader and a universal test. *Duty* is therefore the hinging word. A sense of duty may be carried steadily through the longest life. Duty is the complement of every man's conscience. It calls daily for a conscience void of offence. It has a power such as no potentate on earth can wield. It searches every gap of a man's life. It has a still small voice, but it is persistent and will be heard. It does not call for great things. Rather does it call for little things; and the sting of their neglect is, that they are things the man can do if he will. And if he only will, then he has the spirit of Christ and is one of His.

The trouble with many of us, who would be Christ's, is that we feel bound to aim at great or rare things. Conversion the first thing with many is a great mystery. It is a mystery so great that the life that comes out of it, is regarded as a resurrection from the dead to new impulses, emotions and affections all at once. The will of the man, the conscience of him, and the made up mind—what I have called the sense of duty in him—is no doubt supposed to be involved in the great change. But it does not come to the front as it ought to come, letting love, joy, peace and all the rest follow if, and when they will. Thus and in other ways the test that Scripture propounds first of all for them that are Christ's, runs the risk of being regarded as a secondary demand of His religion.

It is as though God were better pleased with our emotions, our religious hopes and fears and experiences, than He is when calmly and thoughtfully we turn to Him from a sense of duty and with minds deliberately made up to do His will. Far be it from me to say, that He does not love our gratitude and every worthy feeling and emotion of our hearts toward Himself. But He loves these things because He sees in them the buds and beginnings to the keeping of His commandments. And short of this they may die.

Notoriously they often do. But the sense of duty never dies. It lives when hearts grow cold, and faith grows dim, and hope dies out of the heart. Always and evermore there remains, without as with them, the sense of duty, upon which to build up and mature a character which will last till the heavens be no more. On the other hand, doubt and airiness and uncertainty pervade all that does not come out of this everlasting principle of our religion.

It used to be said of the two most powerful nations of the world that the watchword of the one was glory and of the other duty. With the one, France, under the great Napoleon, went forth conquering and to conquer. She enlarged and enriched herself with the spoiling of the nations and became the embodiment of earthly glory. But the glory did not last. It soon turned into a heap of ashes and a name. The glory of France went on to be lost in the shame of an exiled emperor and a bloody revolution. The path of glory ended in a grave.

Meanwhile the lowly word duty gained for England a lasting victory, the fruits of which remain to this day. That word has done its office in anchoring that people to their island dwelling place in peace and prosperity as to a rock in the midst of unstable waters.

And so will duty give us the victory in all our battles of life. It will gain them when all other motive is exhausted and its virtue gone.

Let us take two Scripture illustrations shewing the power of this great principle of Christ's religion in contrast with that of other and lower motives.

Take first, the conduct of the twelve disciples after the death of Lazarus, when it was as much as their lives were worth to go back to Jerusalem. Their impulses of love and affection toward their Master failed them at His words "let us go into Judea again." Hope died down and fear came uppermost. "Master, the Jews of late sought to stone thee, and goest thou thither again?"

Then came His appeal to the sense of duty. "Are there not twelve hours in the day," as though work may or must be done while the day lasts; and so He said, "Our friend Lazarus is dead; let us go to him."

Thomas of all the twelve responded to this call. The sense of duty rose up out of his slow and doubtful and even hopeless heart, "Let us also go that we may die with Him."

And now contrast this exhibition with another in the same company and on another occasion, when Peter was the spokesman out of his eager and impulsive devotion. "Lord I will go with thee to prison and to death." In the one case, Thomas and the sense of duty prevailed and they went. But Peter and hope and impulsive affection failed. And then all the disciples forsook Him and fled.

Let me in conclusion turn to the comfort which comes out of duty done as the test of Christian discipleship.

First to those whose sense of duty, and possibly that alone, is urging them to the Christian life. They have thought that this homely motive is not enough. They need a deeper contrition, more sorrow for sin, more faith, more moving of the Holy Spirit, and more preparation of heart to be Christ's disciples. And so no doubt they do; we all need it. And it is well when we feel the need. What they do feel, however, is that it is their duty to obey the Gospel and live Christian lives. Do they indeed feel this, and do they recognize it as the will of God for them?

That is the question. And for the time they need ask no other. With this let them gird up the loins of their minds and go forward. Dost thou renounce, and dost thou believe? And wilt thou keep the Commandments, and walk in the same all the days of thy life?

To all other questions I may answer in the words of Scripture "If there be first a willing mind, it is accepted according to that a man hath and not according to that he hath not." If any man will do His will, he shall know all he needs to know. Such a one has the spirit of Christ and they who have this are His already. Their sense of duty will keep them following Him to the end of their faith even the salvation of their souls.

There is another class of men and women who need the comfort of this test that they are Christ's. It is they who, acting purely from a sense of duty, have already entered upon the Christian life, and entered it looking perhaps to this day in vain for the joy and hope and peace and assurance on which they counted.

They take a gloomy and desponding view of themselves and their religion. They lack the comfort of its prayers and services. And they fear that their sins are separating between themselves and their God. Does He even will their happiness either here or hereafter?

The question for them to answer is this. Whether among the things they have lost or have never gained there is still left them the sense of duty as a motive and constraint. If that is not lost, then all is not lost. These are Christ's and all things may be theirs. These are the Thomases among His disciples. These are they that fear the Lord, that obey the voice of His servant, yet walk in darkness and have no light.

The word of Scripture to such is one of simple perseverance. It is this, "Let them trust in the name of the Lord, and stay upon their God."

XIII.

ENMITY THROUGH SIN AND RECONCILIATION THROUGH CHRIST—FOR GOOD FRIDAY.

"For if when we were enemies we were reconciled to God by the death of His son; much more, being reconciled, we shall be saved by His life."—Romans v. 10.

THE text brings before us two successive spiritual conditions of ours. First, that of our alienation from God expressed by the words, "when we were enemies"; and second, our reconciliation to Him, "reconciled to God by the death of His son."

These two things, alienation and reconciliation, lie at the foundation of the Christian religion.

First the alienation. For if there be no alienation of man, and no enmity in him to God, then there is no need of reconciliation, and the Gospel of Christ, which on its face and in its tenor and drift is a system of reconciliation, falls to the ground; and there is no need of the life or death of Christ. If He is not a Reconciler of man to God, then He is no more to us than any other good man. In view of

His sufferings and death which the Church is now bringing before us, a feeling of their mysteriousness is apt to take possession of our minds. And questions arise as to their necessity. It is a fit time, therefore, to speak to these questions, and if possible to show where the "needs be" is of the death of Christ our Saviour.

It is not possible, in a single sermon, to do justice to so large a subject as is here brought before us. I will take only a single aspect of it on this occasion. I will regard the alienation or enmity here mentioned of man to God as a thing of growth and of degrees, for the easier understanding of it. Afterwards I will endeavor to show how Christ becomes in His life, and especially in His death, the Reconciler of such enmity to God.

I pray God we may see so much of the truth as will enable us to make an end of all our enmity to Him henceforth, and forevermore. Let me try to illustrate in a familiar way the enmity here indicated. If you come to believe of a neighbor that he is no friend of yours, that belief alone affects your posture of mind toward him. It tends to a coldness of feeling toward him on your part. The common way is for you then to treat him coldly or distantly. That is the first feeling and the first exhibition.

Suppose, however, that you stop short of the exhibition toward him of your coldness. You will say and feel that you are not his enemy. And I admit it. But you will admit, though not his enemy, that you may easily become such. Your coldness or estrangement from him prepares you for it. All that either of you have further to do is to offer some slight, the one to the other, in word, deed or sign, in order to turn your coldness if not into enmity, yet into alienation.

Suppose then further, that you give the first sign of such alienation yourself. You may not thereby turn your neighbor into your enemy. But it is almost inevitable that you should take on a more positive dislike to him. Why? Because you have given him an open sign of unfriendliness, and you cannot suppose him indifferent to it. On the contrary you picture him as provoked by it into a dislike for you. This widens the distance between you, and all by your act or fault. There then you stand as toward your neighbor.

And just there, my dear brethren, we stand or have stood, more or less, toward God. That is the way we get into a state of enmity toward our Maker. Once there, it is hard to get out of it. For, in the first place, we do not see God, or know His posture toward us, any more than in the case supposed we know what is passing in the mind of our neighbor. Our first posture of mind toward God, as toward such a neighbor, may be a mere fancy that God is displeased with us. Then comes the consciousness that we have broken one or more of His commandments. And this consciousness it is that turns our fancy into the sad fact of our enmity to God. It is a helpless result. You may call it the perversity of human nature, and some Christian people, unable to deny the fact, call it natural depravity. We need not worry ourselves over this vexed question. We can see, each one of us for himself, that we become enemies of God in our minds, by wicked works." I have said it is a helpless result. It would not be necessarily helpless in the case supposed between one of us and his neighbor, if that neighbor would speak out at the first sign of coldness given to him on our part, and frankly say, "My dear sir, you are mistaken in supposing I am not your friend. You have been misinformed or you are laboring under a delusion, and here I offer you my hand with my best wishes for your health and happiness." And so as toward God, the enmity might not be a helpless result, if we could see, as in our neighbor, His friendly face, hear His reassuring voice, and go on to find in Him One who is good and gracious, "long suffering and abundant in mercy, forgiving iniquity, transgression and sin."

It may help you to believe that I have given you the truth of the case as it stands, or has stood with most of us, to observe the conduct of a little child toward its parents. The child has done wrong, has been lacking in filial honor, obedience or submission. What is its effect upon himself? Why, following the example of our first father toward God, the child is afraid and hides himself from his own father and mother. He becomes alienated from them in his mind, simply and solely by his own disobedience.

A great deal of fault has been found with the doctrine of natural depravity and original sin. Men object to it. They deny and repudiate it. They challenge us to look childish innocence in the face and call it by any other name. I admit at once that little children are not God's enemies. On the contrary, of such is the Kingdom of Heaven. But if it be true that there is no man that liveth and sinneth not, then there is no child old enough to know good from evil, who does not, from time to time, yield to the inclination of his own will, act against conscience and therefore sin against God. It is hard to go back far enough to know how early a child does this. It is enough to know, in a given case, how early it appears. And no one, child or man, can commit sin without knowing it, and without the conscience that tells him of the Divine displeasure. And just as far as he knows and feels this, he feels alienation, estrangement, and enmity to God.[1] "Enemies in your mind by wicked works." Nothing else makes us enemies of God. And such works are so early and so easy to do, that it is a truth to speak, as the text does, of a time "when we were enemies," as respects the God who made us.

How hard it is to root out enmity, though brought about in this way by yourselves toward a fellow man, you need not be told. He has not wronged you, but you have wronged him or you have slighted him, and so severed on your own side all friendliness and good neighborhood between you. After a season of such severance, it would surprise you to learn of that man, that he had retained any kindness of feeling toward you, or any esteem for your character or ways whatsoever. It is easier for you to believe of a man from whom you had become thus estranged, that he is biding his time to visit you for your wrong, than to picture him, as very possibly he is, without one

[1] Col. i. 21.

particle of hard feeling in return, rejoicing in your prosperity and ready as ever to do you a kindness. So hard is it when coldness has once taken place between friends, to bring it to an end. A first serious difference between them is, of all things, to be dreaded and avoided. It is often the beginning of lifelong estrangements, spreading to families, and handed down to children in inherited animosities.

Now what I say of this everyday working of human nature is, that it is a faithful picture of the spiritual alienation which the Scripture calls "enmity to God." And thus it is that there comes to be a great gulf fixed between man and his Maker.

Thus far then the enmity. I turn to the Reconciliation. Much that has been said and written on this subject proceeds upon the idea that the chief, if not the sole need of reconciliation, is on God's side, not ours; and that here is the great virtue of Christ's death as an atonement. We say indeed that God is offended, that He is provoked, even as the Scripture declares and that He is angry with the wicked. The literal, rather than the figurative truth of all this gets itself fastened in the sinner's mind; and it does not strike him as strange, although the alienation and the enmity are in fact all on his own side.

It follows therefore that Christ came, so far as we are concerned with His coming, to bridge the gulf by which we may return to God, rather than that by which God may come to us.

We may safely leave that Almighty Being to the vindication of His own character and ways. If He be indeed God, He is immutable. He changes not. The sun shines on though cloud and mist may rise on earth to obscure His shining to us. We may not see the light or feel the heat. And yet the sun shines on in His place in the heavens. And so God is Light and in Him is no darkness at all. Only to the sinner conscious of his sins, He is not light but darkness and He is not love but coldness and displeasure.

What then I ask must be the great work of a Reconciler of man to God? It is to brush away the clouds and scatter the darkness in which we stand here on earth, and which are intercepting the love and light which God is, so that hope and warmth may spring up and glow in cold, alienated human hearts, melt the enmity that is in them into streams of confiding trust and returning love and obedience to the Lord our God.

If the figure I have used here is a true representation, we can understand how Christ becomes our Reconciler unto God. First and foremost He came among us that we might, to use the apostle's carefully chosen and intelligible words, "see in Him the express image of God's person," and give that image place in our thoughts, where otherwise stands imaged a face set against us in a cold, unchanging frown of displeasure and dislike. The face now appearing there is the face of a Friend and a Brother.

Moreover His coming into the world was no burst of sunshine on a cloudy day, warming the world for a moment out of its coldness and darkness, its fear of God and its enmity toward Him, only to settle back upon it as darkly as ever. But the Son of God "was made Flesh and dwelt among us, and we beheld His glory, the glory of the only begotten of the Father, full of grace and truth." His was a sun that shone on for three and thirty years here among us, and shone to the last, full orbed and without a cloud between Him and the souls He came to save.

I go on to say that the life of Christ, precious as it was, and clearly as it manifested forth a God of love and mercy, was not alone sufficient to break down the partition wall of man's inveterate alienation. We have seen how easily a feeling of distrust is engendered against a fellow man to whom we have shown a coldness.

Hardly can he after that, by turning toward us however kindly a face, smile that coldness away. Something further is needed. Something that costs him more, and is more reassuring to us. In short what we want is assurance in some way from him, that our offence is forgiven and forgotten.

And here comes in the need to us of the death of Christ. In sacrifice there is a force and meaning that cannot be mistaken. In sacrifice for our sakes, there is a virtue to heal the wound and close the gap of the widest enmity and alienation. The hardest and the coldest heart will yield to suffering on its behalf. The murmurings of dislike are dumb at last before the pouring out, for our sakes, of the lifeblood of our Reconciler unto God.

Look for a moment at that tremendous sacrifice. First and foremost God there gave the best and dearest He had to give. " This is my beloved Son." And He gave it at its best. " Here," as one has said,[1] " was the sacrifice of a life, neither in early youth nor in advanced years, and the man who sacrifices the strongest, noblest life of which humanity is capable, must die with terrible effort. He must struggle in death with the highest energies of life."

And this beloved Son was not only given to

[1] Canon Liddon.

death at His best, He was given to death at its worst. " Even the death of the Cross." So that the pure, strong and noble life of our Redeemer was wrung out of Him by a protracted torture.

My dear brethren : It was His willingness so to die. It is the largeness, nay the lavishness of His sacrifice that bridges the gulf between man and God so that a gulf no longer appears.

We cannot contemplate so tremendous an event in human history as this, and wonder at scarcely any blessed result that is claimed for it. The earthquake shock of Christ's expiring breath vibrates, at this commemorative season of His Church, through all the distance and lapse of time and space that lie between the Calvary of the first, and the America of this nineteenth century. And the inspired words that describe its results and consequences then and there, are no faint or distant echo in our ears to-day.

Listen to the words that describe it—" He is our peace who hath made both one, and hath broken down the middle wall of partition between us "—Again : " that He might reconcile both unto God in one body by the cross, having slain the enmity thereby." And yet again, " And you being dead in your sins, hath He quickened together with Him, blotting out the handwriting that was against us, and nailing it to His cross."

Can it be needful to go further to show the power of a Reconciliation like this. The words of our text are enough. "If when we were enemies we were reconciled to God by the death of His son, much more being reconciled shall we be saved by His life?"

I close with one more triumphant challenge of the New Testament,

"If God spared not His own Son, but freely delivered Him up for us all, how shall He not, with Him, freely give us all things."

XIV.

INCREDIBLE ALTERNATIVES TO THE RESURRECTION OF THE DEAD—FOR EASTER DAY.

" For if the dead rise not, then is Christ not raised : and if Christ be not raised your faith is vain—ye are yet in your sins. Then they also that are fallen asleep in Christ are perished."—1 Cor. xv. 16, 17, 18.

THIS chapter has become familiar, not so much for what it is, a chapter of reasons and illustrations in favor of the resurrection of the body, but rather as a requiem over bodies committed to the ground, earth to earth, ashes to ashes, and dust to dust. It has thus been made to speak to the heart rather than to the head.

Its final note is as though our night had come to a sunburst. " O grave where is thy victory ? " It is a note that we often falter forth in anguish of spirit. We break down with the feeling that death has its sting for the living if not for the dying. But there is no incongruity in this mingled feeling. With burdened hearts and streaming eyes, we can yet thank God who giveth us the victory through our Lord Jesus Christ. Out of the swollen tide of grief, hope rises and drops her anchor, all the more deeply, into the cleft rock. Even with the dread image of Job before our eyes, of worms destroying this body, we may yet break forth as he did with the assurance "I know that my Redeemer liveth."

On this day I will simply ask you to let this chapter speak forth some of the calm and solid reasons it has to give, for our faith in the resurrection of the body. Such reasons we shall want in our trial hour. It is a hard Article of the Creed to believe. There are those who would be glad to believe it, but who say they cannot. They can believe in Jesus Christ. That is they can accept Him in His life and death, but they hesitate when it comes to the rising from the dead. Like the disciples before the fact, they inquire among themselves to this day, what the rising from the dead should mean.

Let me speak to such and to all, in some of the thoughts and considerations of this chapter. St. Paul here leads to his sure and certain hope of the resurrection of the dead, through a series of incredible alternatives. And what are they?

The first is that if the dead rise not, then Christ is not risen. He cannot view the two things, Christ's resurrection and ours apart from one another; and this because Christ in His teaching never did. He foretold His own resurrection with the addition always expressed or implied, " Because I live, ye shall live also." And that Christ was not risen, was to the apostle an incredible thing—incredible because so many people saw Him with their own eyes, who knew Him before His death—first Cephas then James, and then the rest of the apostles. He was seen besides of five hundred brethren at once, most of whom were living when this chapter was written. And he goes on to name one more witness, the writer of this chapter, St. Paul himself. He had seen the risen Jesus by a lightning flash from heaven, and was carrying the marks of that vision in his eyes at that moment, and carried them to the end of his life. Do not hastily pass the testimony of this eyewitness of the risen Jesus. He had not indeed seen Christ till he saw Him risen from the dead. But this whole chapter moves in an atmosphere of truth.

There is an earnestness and an outspokenness in it that show the writer penetrated by a deep and thorough conviction—a conviction that carried him through a long and painful life to a martyr's death. And St. Paul is an independent witness. He had not accepted the testimony of the twelve, but rejected it with an incredulity that amounted to scorn and contempt.

He set out for Damascus to put down the imposture of this pretended resurrection. It was then and there that the risen Lord encountered him face to face. His conversion turned upon the fact that he had seen the Lord, and from a frenzied disbeliever he became, from that moment, the foremost believer of them all, in Jesus and the Resurrection.

So with all the chosen witnesses. They not only proclaimed it, but lived out their belief in it, as St. Paul did, even to prison and to death. They all believed their Lord was risen from the dead. You cannot doubt that. And those who heard their testimony were convinced by it, and we have their witness, and that of the generations following handed down to this day, in the Church visible before our eyes. The Church is founded upon the testimony of these men as its corner stone. The Holy Church throughout the world has acknowledged from that day to this, the glorious resurrection. Is it credible that these men were false witnesses of God, who sealed their testimony with their blood, and that the rock on which was built the Church, and on which it firmly stands to-day, was built upon a lie and not the truth? It is not credible.

Another incredible alternative of this chapter is that our faith is vain, and we are yet in our sins. You may ask how this follows if Christ be not risen. Understand that the faith of which the apostle speaks is reliance on the efficacy of Christ's death as an atonement for the sins of men. If Christ be not risen, His death was in vain, with all its pain and agony and shame. Why? Because we can never know that the death of Christ has any virtue in it. Its virtue to us depends on our belief in its acceptance with God. And if Christ be not risen, then God has not accepted it, or if He has, we can never be certified of the fact, and so our faith falls to the ground. Is this credible? Is it possible that that wonderful birth, announced from heaven by an angel, and that holy, harmless and undefiled life, and that cross and passion at the end of it, all looking to a rising again for our justification, have gone emptied of all their meaning, into a returnless grave? It is not possible. And yet it is true if Christ be not raised.

There is another way in which we may be said to be in our sins with a vain or an uninfluential faith, if Christ be not risen. What we need is motive strong enough to rise from sin to newness of life. Take away the resurrection from the dead, and where is that motive?

I know there are people who think they can be virtuous for virtue's sake. They dream of a goodness that has its only spring in the wish to live a good life, and to leave a good name behind them, for the sake of posterity. But what is a good name, or what is posterity, to one who has no hope for himself or his posterity beyond the grave, where no mention of them more is heard of? Weak is the motive to live and labor for the future good of beings who are to sink to-morrow into nothingness. And of what avail is a good example, if there be no assurance of any other life than these short uncertain years of earth? No. "If the dead rise not, let us eat and drink for to-morrow we die." That is the one rational alternative. There is no adequate motive left to doing or daring a hard or a self-sacrificing, or a humiliating thing, as St. Paul did. "What advantageth it me if I have fought with beasts at Ephesus, if the dead rise not?" And will a man think it credible that God should set before him no adequate motive to living the righteous and godly life, that the same God and his own conscience combine to tell him he ought to live? It is incredible.

I pass on to the final incredibility named in the text. "Then they also that are fallen asleep in Christ are perished."

St. Paul here sends the doubters and deniers to the mouldering remains of those righteous men, who serving God in their day and generation, have died missing all adequate compensation on earth. Let me try to show you what this incredibility is by two illustrations.

The first I will take from the lives of those of old time, and of whom the Old Testament Scripture speaks. Take Abraham and those who followed in the faith of this patriarch. He left his native land relying on the promise of God of an inheritance in some other for himself and his seed. Was it the land of Canaan? So he thought when he left his own country and found the land whither he went. But what was the result? God gave Abraham "none inheritance in that land, no not so much as to set his foot on." It is distinctly said of him that he "sojourned in the land of promise as in a strange land." To Abraham, therefore, if we thus interpret the promise, it never was fulfilled. Nor was it to his descendants. Jacob and his sons found the promise an illusion. Hardly had they made their home there, when a famine drove them out of it into the land of Egypt. There they lived and died, they and their children, for four hundred years. The promise of an inheritance glorious in its terms, shrunk in the land of Palestine to a small patch and possession of a burying place in it for these men of faith.

And then again Moses. What was the upshot of the promise to that glorious leader and three millions of his people, when at last they returned from Egypt to take possession of that land. They found themselves in a wilderness where they wandered forty years, and where their carcasses fell, from the greatest of them, Moses himself, to the humblest believer in the promises of God. The incredible thing here is, that God made a promise to the ear and broke it to the hope of all these generations. The thing is impossible. And then what follows? Why, that there remaineth yet a land that can and will be handed over to the faithful departed, by a true and faithful God; a land in which, according to the promise, they will hunger no more, neither thirst any more and where neither the sun shall light on them nor any heat. And so they came to understand and to interpret it. It is declared that "all these died in faith, not having received the promise, and confessed that they were strangers and pilgrims on the earth." Even in death they counted Him faithful that promised. What then shall we say, when it comes to the question whether these that have fallen asleep in Christ are perished? Perish the thought!

Take another case nearer home. Call to mind departed saints of God whom you have known, and hold to-day in sacred and loving remembrance. Men and women they were who have missed all earthly reward or compensation for their lives of faith and unselfish service of others, missing the outward comforts of this life—the blessing even of health of body denied them. Life has proved to them a series of losses and disappointments. In the judgment of the world they go to the grave having lost the life that now is. And yet their fear of God, and faith in Christ, were strong enough to enable them to submit cheerfully to their lot of toil and poverty and infirmity, and to wear out their lives in the service of family or friends and even of strangers, while all around them they had to see the rewards of earth carried off by the high hand, the bold front, and the selfish determination of people to make their lives successes here. Of these last we may say, "They have their reward." But where is the reward of the unselfish, suffering faithful servants of God and man, to the end of their lives here on earth? That which only bears them up through life, is the belief that there is reserved for them a future beyond the grave,

"Where they shall dwell as children,
Who here as exiles mourn."

These that have fallen asleep in Christ perished? It is incredible, unless it is credible that there is no righteous judge of all the earth.

I leave the factors, well known and patent, of such a problem as this, to be pondered by you who are before me. But before I close I will give you the inevitable inference of St. Paul as it stands at the opening of the burial lesson. "But now is Christ risen from the dead and become the first-fruits of them that slept."

I give also the closing, and to us who are living, the practical and concerning portion of this great chapter.

"Wherefore, my beloved brethren, be ye steadfast, unmovable, always abounding in the work of the Lord. Forasmuch as ye know that your labor is not in vain in the Lord."

XV.

GRIEVING THE SPIRIT—
FOR WHITSUNDAY.

"Grieve not the Holy Spirit of God whereby ye are sealed unto the day of Redemption."—Eph. iv. 30.

BY whom ye are sealed. In the original that is the word instead of whereby. It is one among the many Scripture tokens of the personality of the Holy Ghost. But there is other and better evidence of the personality of the Spirit in the words—Grieve not. This attributes personal qualities to the Holy Spirit in no other or different way than it attributes them to one of ourselves. It is not however with a view to proving the personality of the third person of the blessed Trinity that I have chosen these words for a text on this day sacred to Him. The text contains an expostulation addressed to those who have been made Christians by the sealing ordinance of the New Testament—the laying on of hands. It warns them not to sin against a loving, sensitive Being. It is an appeal to that which feels in our own breasts, rather than to the conscience or in-

intellect. It speaks in the use of words that wake up the tenderness of our hearts, and our consideration for the feelings of another. We are indeed to beware of resisting or striving against the influence of the Holy Spirit vouchsafed to us for our own sakes—for the sake of conscience and duty, in view of the risk we run of being forsaken of that influence. But what this Scripture seems to say is that we resist not the Holy Spirit for His sake. Grieve not the Holy Spirit of God. And the word Grieve shall be the keynote of what I shall try to say on this occasion.

In the common case of appeals made to that which is tender, sympathetic, and considerate for others in our human nature, our hearts respond and that instinctively, if we respond at all. We do not stop to think, and hardly do we reason with such appeals. We obey a quicker, an easier and a more constraining and powerful impulse than that of the conscience or the reason. We act in accordance with our sensitive nature, when we take counsel not of our heads, but of our hearts. It is easier to act with such an impulse behind us, because we are thus relieved of a burden whose pressure we feel more quickly than we feel that of conscience or a sense of duty. And I need not say that we require the ready help of every worthy instinct we have to the bracing of our weak natures in the line of duty.

When then the apostle warns us not to grieve the Holy Spirit, by whom we are sealed, he means that such treatment is an unfeeling return for the boon we have received and the help that is offered us by the Holy Spirit of God. And why unfeeling unless it is an occasion of suffering to a benefactor? If there is no heartfelt response on our part to this appeal, it must be because we regard the slight, the grief, the suffering of the Holy Spirit, as a mere figure of speech, and no real slight or grief or suffering. If we stop to reason coldly upon such language of Scripture as this, we may say that God does not nor can he truly be said to feel or to suffer. And if He is spoken of as grieved or sorrowing over the dishonor we do Him, it is only meant that He treats us as though He were. Such reasoning as this takes all virtue out of the instinct it appeals to in our sensitive hearts as the most quickly responsive one we have, and it takes all power if not all meaning out of words. If words in Scripture do not mean substantially what they say, where is the power attributed to Scripture of a two-edged sword. It is no sword at all in human hands or human hearts. It is powerless over the strongest motives that are in us. If you have done a wrong or a dishonor to an utterly impassive personage, or to no person at all in grieving the Holy Spirit of God, what, I ask, can be appealed to in us with any hope that we will refrain from that wrong or repent of it? Nothing is left with which to prick the heart with a sense of guilt or unworthiness. And we must be left to consult only our own sense of duty and propriety. The slow moving and comparatively feeble incentives to right doing and right living become no incentive at all where passion or inclination is moving the other way. No. Your hearts must be touched by a sense of the injury, the wrong, the suffering you are inflicting, and then only is there the hope of that change of heart and affection which religion contemplates.

Here is the motive power of the Gospel notwithstanding all that may be said of an impassive Deity. That idea of an unsuffering God may be carried too far. When He solemnly declares to me that He made me in His own image and likeness, I look within for what may answer to that likeness. And when I find there among other elements of my nature something of tenderness and sensitiveness and delicacy of feeling, and something of the sympathy and consideration for others which distinguish me from the brutes that perish, I will believe that these are among the traits and the lineaments that remain to me of the image of God in which I was created. And I will cherish them and give them life and scope and activity, not only toward my fellow man but toward Him whose gift they are, as though they were all alive and working in Him, their Author and their Giver.

You will understand then that I take these words of the inspired apostle, to mean what they say; and that requires that we take the Holy Spirit of God in the first place as a personal Being; and then as a person who feels— feels slights and wrongs and the sting of ingratitude and has a sense of the dishonor done to Him.

My dear brethren, the delusion under which men labor of having to do only with a cold, impassive Deity, and which they are acting out in their lives, comes of their disbelieving or ignoring the Divinity of Christ, and casting out of the Godhead all that is purely human as not belonging there. Or if not this, then they let go the idea of His humanity where He is at the right hand of God. They imagine Him sitting there divested of it, lifted altogether away from themselves, with nothing in common with us left any more in Him. And they regard the third person in the blessed Trinity only as a cold ethereal, unembodied influence or effluence of God. We are orthodox in our confession of His personality, but the mass of us are prone to live and move and have our religious being in this world, as though we were alone in it. We may have occasional touches as from a heavenly source, arousing conscience and stirring the will to duty, but with the human heart and affections left out. Is that, indeed, all we are to believe of the Holy Spirit of God? If so, then there may be light from heaven shining for us. But where is the heat? We need that even more than we need light. Light enough we have. But who of us acts up to his light? Who among us does as well as he knows? Alas, not one! We must be moved to acting out the light and the faith that are in us. And what we need for this is a present Saviour, who can be pleased or grieved, honored or dishonored, and feel the pleasure or the grief, the honor or the dishonor. We need to feel that we are not left alone to struggle with a sinful nature in a sinful world. Power, indeed, there would be if the Saviour in whom we believe were body and soul here with us in all the sympathy, sensitiveness, solicitude and compassion that He had for those who knew Him here in the flesh. But why can we not have this presence and this power? Is it because He in person cannot be at all times and in all places where His scattered people stand? Did He not provide for this when He coupled the words "It is expedient for you that I go away" with the assurance that He would not leave us comfortless, and that He would come to us. What or who then, I ask, must be the Spirit whom He sent, but the Spirit in and through whom He comes, as He said He would, to abide with us forever? We cannot, and God be thanked we need not, in view of such assurances as these, sever the humanity of Christ from the Spirit whom He sent down from heaven as on this day. In so many words He is called the Spirit of the Son. And so it is that He accomplishes those precious words, the last before he left the earth, "Lo, I am with you alway even unto the end of the world." They are true words only in and through His Holy Spirit.

And now look again at the words of the text—"Grieve not the Holy Spirit of God"—and you will see that they point to the human, the feeling, and the suffering side of our blessed Saviour Himself. To His grieved Holy Spirit He may truly say, "The reproaches of them that reproached Thee fell upon me." Our neglectful treatment of that Spirit touches an electric cord which has a human Saviour at the end of it. His are the joy and the grief, the sorrow and the jealousy that are spoken of God and His Holy Spirit. I know we say and think of Christ, that His sufferings were ended and done, when He declared on the cross that it was finished. But what was finished there? The one sacrifice for sin was finished with the suffering that belonged to that, so that there remaineth no more sacrifice for sin—and He sat down on the right hand of God. But was His work then finished? and does He sit there with no more thought for us and no more care? Does He contemplate with no more of human feeling and no more solicitude the outcome of His work on earth? Does He survey with cold indifference from the serene height whereon He sits the toils and struggles of His people or the slights and neglects that go on, of the salvation wrought out for the world He once loved even unto death? God forbid! His Spirit maketh intercession for them with groanings that cannot be uttered. There is joy in heaven over one sinner that repenteth. He sees in that repentance the travail of His soul and is satisfied. All this is as true of Him now as in the days of His flesh. Let us rid ourselves then of the idea that all this present working of the divine humanity set forth in Scripture is a mere figure of speech. Let us understand that our sins and shortcomings and neglects, our slights of the monitor within the breast, have in them stings for Him who laid down His life in order to turn hearts of stone into hearts of flesh and blood. He who redeemed us to God by His blood neither leaves nor forsakes those whom He has sealed by His Holy Spirit unto the day of redemption.

Again and finally. Let us remember that in grieving the Holy Spirit we may go so far as to "quench the Spirit." If we pause to think one moment, there must be such a thing. Yes. There may be such a persistent turning away from Him that speaketh from heaven that he will speak no more. That posture of ours must at last be accepted as a final and determined rejection of Him and a refusal to listen to His voice. How can he save us if He would, when He has to say to us, "I have called and ye refused, I have stretched out my hand and no man regarded, but ye have set at naught all my counsel and would none of my reproof"—God forbid that any one here should incur the doom of being left alone of the Holy Spirit of God.

XVI.

THE THREEFOLD NAME—
FOR TRINITY SUNDAY.

"Go ye therefore and teach all nations, baptizing them in the name of the Father, and of the Son, and of the Holy Ghost."—St. Matt. xxviii. 19.

IN these words of Christ is contained the germinal faith of Christianity. The word Creed, in the vocabulary of our religion, is a word against which no little modern thought has been directed, as though it ought to be relegated to the realm of old and worn-out things. Here, however, is expressed something, call it what you will, which explicitly requires, not the mere assent, but the submission of all who would be Christ's disciples. They must accept His Name. And here is the Name by which He has chosen to be called. It is impossible to avoid acknowledging this name by calling Him, as some do, a Reformer, or as others do, without defining what they mean, a Saviour and a Redeemer.

In the words before us is a threefold Name, which the Reformer, Saviour and Redeemer, and He was indeed all these, has first of all and above all, taken to Himself, and provided that it shall be stamped by the initial rite of His religion upon all His followers. If any man then would answer in the fewest words, what the faith of Christianity is, he must answer with these words or take them as the foundation of what he believes. And so there must needs be a Creed, if Christianity is to be anything beyond a varying sentiment of religion, gathered how or where every man shall choose for himself. These words constitute the basis of a Creed. I may say that in fact they grew up into the creed of the Church as it stands to-day, and that early enough in its history to be not misnamed "the Apostles' Creed." This creed was really handed to them in their final commission, and in the terms now before us. A Christian without this creed, must in the contemplation of Christ, be an anomaly. A condemnation of Creeds by one who calls himself a Christian is therefore a condemnation of himself, unless he saves himself by holding fast to this form of words by some other name.

It needs no apology, my brethren, at any time, to speak to a Christian congregation in behalf of their Creed, and especially at a time like this, when doubt and obscurity are thrown, not only about the necessity or importance of a

Creed, but on one after another truth contained in or necessarily growing out of the formula now before us. In this Church the day has come round in the calendar for the grand logical summing up of the year's doctrinal teachings, and for the intelligent confession by our congregations of a "true faith." That faith is called in two words, the "Eternal Trinity." It is not a Scripture word, but it is an intelligible synonym for the Name spread out in the formula of Baptism.

One additional remark before proceeding to the subject before us. Setting light by creeds, and putting above and in opposition to them, the conduct of the life is not a novel feature of our day. It was more bluntly than poetically said, two hundred years ago,

"For modes of faith let senseless bigots fight,
His creed cannot be wrong whose life is in the right."

It is more politely said in our day, but that is all the advance that has been made in two hundred years, by the men who would away with creeds. Their meaning is the same. And that meaning, word it as you will, is delusive and false. A creed, or a faith, is as needful a start for right conduct, or a right life in man, as a spinal column is needful to right life in an animal.

A right life requires a right motive behind it, and that motive is a man's belief, in other words, his creed. A motiveless or a creedless life is an aimless and a worthless life. It is the right motive, the right belief, the right Creed, out of which comes a life that is " in the right." It can come in no other way.

And thus in insisting upon the necessity of a Creed in religion, we are simply and only insisting upon an adequate motive to a religious life. And in further insisting upon a right creed we are insisting upon that without which no man can go on to live a right life in the sight of God. Some men refuse to be bound as they call it, by creeds, in the fear that they may outgrow them, that their creed will prove too small for their growing and expanding knowledge, and that what they believe to-day may be upset by what their own or some other man's thought or investigation may discover to-morrow.

Such an assumption as this is founded in the mistake that a creed is a chain of logical or philosophical reasoning, and a thing of human framing, or a series of interpretations of the Scripture. Whereas, it is simply a matter of fact and of testimony. Our Lord declared what a creed is when He said to Nicodemus, " We speak that we do know and testify that we have seen, and ye received not our witness." They who receive not such witness are the rejecters and the slighters of creeds.

And now what is the Creed, in other words the true faith of the Christian religion? If we look into the Acts of the Apostles under the final commission of their master, we shall know what they believed, from seeing what they did.

The first thing they did was to call on the thousands gathered out of every nation under heaven at the feast of Pentecost, to repent and be baptized every one of them in the name of Jesus Christ for the remission of sins, with the assurance to them that they should receive the Holy Ghost. They repented accordingly and they were baptized in the name of Christ, and that was the threefold name which the apostles and their converts received on His testimony of what He knew and had seen. For He only knew God and had seen Him.

And so it is declared of these thousands and of all others who went on to be baptized by the apostles, that they believed. Believed what? Believed first and foremost in the Threefold Name into which they were baptized, and believed it on the testimony of Christ Himself; believed next in the forgiveness of their sins on the same testimony; believed thirdly that they had received the Holy Ghost as promised by

Him, and believed that with the Holy Ghost they had received some virtue, more or less, for living a righteous life. How much more they believed, or how distinctly they believed this, we do not know. How clearly they ascribed the virtue of the forgiveness of their sins to the name of Christ, or that of their new life to the Holy Ghost, we cannot tell. But here, in the Threefold Name, was contained the truth that they believed and upon which they acted. You cannot doubt this.

Here then is the foundation, and no little of the superstructure with it, of the Christian faith. And other foundation can no man lay than that which is laid. The superstructure which man builds may be wrong. He may build, and I do not deny that there have been built up creeds, so called, of hay and stubble whose end is that they shall be burned. Man's opinions and Scripture glosses have been added. Platforms have been constructed out of the Scriptures, and possibly outside the Scriptures, and called creeds. And they may be justly liable to the condemnation that is being cast in these days indiscriminately upon creeds. I do not stand here in defence of any one of them, or of any creed or doctrine of the Christian religion, but that which comes fairly out of the formula of baptism and the acts and teachings of the men having that formula in charge. It was His final charge to them by their Lord and Master, for the nations of the earth.

I need not say that questions have arisen upon the meaning of this formula, plain as that meaning seems to be. A meaning has been put upon it which deprives the second Person named in it of His essential divinity, reducing Him to a mere, however extraordinary, human being; and the third has been deprived of all separate personality, and reduced to the level of an attribute or quality or mere effluence of Deity.

Now if we are right in saying that a right life depends on a right or a true creed, here at the hinge and centre of all religious truth, a mistake or a misapprehension must of all others be the most disastrous. I would ask the man then who so reads this formula, where in it is the virtue or where any assurance whatever, of the forgiveness of sins? With a man, and no more than a man, for a Redeemer, what man is free to live a right life, untrammeled of all fear from his past sins, or with such a hope for the future as may support him through all dangers and carry him through all temptations? Such a hope must enter into that within the vail, and be an anchor of the soul both sure and steadfast. Or where, on the other hand, is the steady presence in the breast, of an indwelling guest from heaven, who will never leave nor forsake the Christian believer, assuring him that he is never alone while he lives or when he dies, and whose work is needful evermore,

> "To cleanse the heart,
> To sanctify the soul,
> To pour fresh life in every part,
> And new create the whole."

But however hopeful or however tolerable a righteous life may promise to be, as issuing out of a creed with a Redeemer who, whatever He is, has not an arm like God, nor a single Divine prerogative of His own to sustain him, or, how much comfort through life or in death, may come out of the influence of a God afar off, I stand here, my brethren, to say that such a God is not our God, nor the God of the Christian ages. It would seem that to a mind unprejudiced and unprepossessed, and at all open to conviction, the formula of baptism, as it fell from the lips of Christ upon the ears of His apostles, is so worded that it not only implies but asserts the doctrine of the eternal Trinity, which the Church this day commemorates and adores.

Trinitarians and Unitarians alike will admit that the Deity is named in this formula. If not, then the formula is simply unaccountable. But how and where in it is the Supreme Being named? On the hypothesis that the Son is not that Being and no part of it, nor the Holy Ghost, where is the name of God, or the equivalent of His name to be found in these words? It is not found there. For the Father is not God here, except as the second person named is the Son, and you must join the two to give the name of Deity to the words. On the hypothesis that the second is not the name of a Divine person, the formula would have had different wording. It would have expressed the name of the One Divine Being, distinctly and separately, in order to forbid its being confounded, either with that of the Son or the Holy Ghost.

The Higher would be first fully named, and then the lower. The formula would then be, "in the name of God the Father, and in the name of Jesus Christ the Son." But no, it stands "in the name," singular number, and not names, " of the Father and of the Son and of the Holy Ghost," all one name. " The formula runs along," to use the words of another, "in a style perfectly equal and familiar without any note of distinction or difference, more than that of personal relation carrying with it the idea of sameness of nature." He might have added, that it excludes the idea of any difference of nature in the use of the singular, Name.

But again: Here is a formula which may be called the door of entrance into the kingdom of heaven so far as the Church on earth is that kingdom. It is used at the turning point for every Christian believer. The words used in it are those by which He is sworn to allegiance and brought into covenant with His Maker.

On the hypothesis that the Threefold Name is any more or any less than the Name of God Himself, it is an indignity to that great Being who declares that He will not give His glory to another.

What an awful impertinence, in the most solemn act of his human creatures, it must be to couple the name of their Creator with that of a creature of His hand! It is, in effect, raising to the throne of the human affections where God should sit alone, and coupling with Him there, a creature of God, however lofty, or however honored, or worthy, yet a creature if not Himself Divine.

The first and great commandment is, that we have no other Gods before Him. And here in the covenant of Baptism is the first open act of worship, adoration, and submission we pay to Him. We thus enter His Kingdom on earth, and we look first of all to see Him, or to know Him who He is; and what we find on the threshold is His name coupled and associated with one or more other beings, in such a way that we cannot so much as name Him, without at the same time naming them. We cannot say, we believe in Him without saying that we believe in them. Strangely called reasonable is that religion, which requires its believers, or allows them, to be baptized in the name of God, and at the same moment in the name of a creature, and in the name of an attribute; into the faith of two persons, one infinite, another finite, and of a third without even personality to justify its position, at the door of entrance into the Kingdom of God.

The doctrine of the blessed Trinity may be charged with incomprehensibility, and that is the heaviest stumbling-block that can be placed in the way of believing it. But any other resolution into its elements, of the formula before us, discloses a contradiction so irreconcilable, a confusion so inextricable, and an absurdity so awful, that to find in it the doctrine of "Three Divine Persons, and one only God," is so profound a relief, that we may bless Him who has given unto us His servants "grace, by the confession of a true faith, to acknowledge the glory of the eternal Trinity, and in the power of the Divine Majesty to worship the

Unity, and" to beseech Him, to "keep us steadfast in this faith, who lives and reigns One God, world without end."

The question of Creed came not long ago into unusual prominence among us. Two large bodies of Christians, this Church and the Presbyterian body, have been forced to action upon that question. In one it assumed the form of a question of revision as respects their confession of faith, and that is their creed. In this Church its short, plain and comprehensive creed of the apostles was called in question by one of her ministry seriously enough to have resulted in his deposition. Others of his brethren had become involved in the suspicion of a like unsoundness in this faith. These men have been falling back upon some new and phantom interpretation of the Scripture, which will allow the words of the creed to stand, and yet evacuates them of the miraculous and the mysterious, which the Church from the beginning, and the vast body of her ministry and membership at this day, accept without a doubt or a question as the truth of God. The Incarnation of Christ is one of these miracles or mysteries thus pared down by the new reading of the Scripture. His resurrection from the dead is another.

In view of the formula of baptism to which

your attention has now been called and its plain, indeed I may say its inevitable meaning, we may well insist that the disbelievers and the doubters of the Incarnation and the Resurrection have a first work to do. They seem to think it enough to bring new interpretations of Scripture to their aid in the work of demolishing the creed. Let them give their attention first and foremost to the formula of Baptism as it fell from the lips of Christ Himself. Here and not in the creed the great mystery and the great miracle of our religion consist. It is placed by the Head of the Church at the door of His Church. If that fact does not lie as an obstacle in the way of men's entering there; if they can go in "in the Name of the Father and of the Son and of the Holy Ghost," it is comparatively a little and an easy thing to believe, that Jesus Christ our Lord was conceived of the Holy Ghost, born of the Virgin Mary, and rose again from the dead.

The question rather is: How was He *not* all the creed declares Him to be?

In view of this mystery on the threshold of our religion we may truly say, Without controversy great is the mystery of God, whose Name indeed is Wonderful, Counsellor, the Mighty God, the Everlasting Father, the Prince of Peace.

XVII.

CHRISTIANITY AN EMBODIED AND UNCHANGEABLE RELIGION.

"Jesus Christ the same yesterday, to-day and forever."—Hebrews xiii. 8.

THE doctrine of this Scripture is opposed to much of the thinking and the impressions of Christianity that prevail. The doctrine of the text is that through all the past, present and future of this world's history Jesus Christ is the same. His religion must therefore be also the same unchanged and unchangeable. And so the exhortation "Be not ye carried about with divers and strange doctrines."

The changes and advances of knowledge have changed our modes of life and thought to an extent that would astonish a man of the first five centuries of Christianity. Could our fathers of a century ago revisit the earth they would learn much of which they were profoundly ignorant, and they would have to unlearn much that they thought they knew.

The reformation of the sixteenth century gave a jar to Christendom that seemed to loosen historical Christianity from its foundations. There was enough of unsettlement and unhingement brought about by it to open the door to the question whether Christianity should not share in the reformations, improvements and developments that have been going on in every other department of human knowledge. Whatever of good came out of that religious upheaval, it seems to have opened the door to questions of the most radical kind. Is the Church of Christ identical with a visible and historical body of believers? Is such a body a necessity by any law of Christ? What is the theory of Christianity? Are creeds and sacraments a necessary part of it, or are they its accidents?

At any rate, these are the questions now, and the starting of them within the pale of the Church has given encouragement to the free thought that is gradually tending to the conclusion that the religion of Christ is a sentiment rather than a Creed or an Institution. That idea is in harmony with the changing character of the age. It enables men to accommodate their religion to the fluctuations of opinion around them, letting it take its hue from each of them in turn. It is insisted that only so can Christianity adapt itself to the advancing intelligence of the human race and the varying demands of human society. And so it is thought to be doing the religion of Christ the greatest possible service to get it out of its hide-bound creeds and the narrowness of a visible body, and to shake it loose from its effete traditions and the formalism of its ordinances. In this way every man will be free to believe in his ideal Christ, even if that ideal be no more than the soothing, pleasing thought of a man who walked the earth at peace with God, and in perfect charity with the world and succumbed at last to an agonizing death without a murmur, and without an explanation that bound His followers to anything in particular. The statement is ascribed to a late distinguished preacher,—not of this Church,—that "the disintegration of old religious forms begun at the Reformation, has been going on in such a way that at last it is admitted that men have a right to hold their own views, and that there is no power to determine what shall be the faith of the Churches or sects." This preacher was a close observer of the drift of public opinion, whether religious or secular. He declared that we live in an age of Christian sympathy, as never before, and he ascribes it to the closer contact of nations and peoples, brought about by the aid of steam and electricity. And he anticipates the blessedness which is coming more and more in this way to the nations of the earth.

Such is the idea of Christ's religion that satisfies him, and it is an idea that prevails where there is no preacher and no Church and no Lord's day, and where the traditions and ordinances of Christianity are openly given up and abandoned. Let me say here that I do not deny the prevalence of Christian sympathy, nor that it is growing among Christian nations. What I do deny is that that result is due to the sentimental Christianity of this preacher. To another sort of Christianity, as I shall endeavor to show, are we indebted for all that is blessed in Christian sympathy, and for all that is valuable in Christian civilization.

Planting myself on the doctrine of the words before us, I lay it down that the Christianity that stood in the conception of its Divine Author before He came into the world, is the Christianity that was wrought out by Him when He came,—in other words,—that the New Testament unfolded the Christ and His gospel which were enfolded in the Old; and what they were, we are able to say beyond a doubt. The priesthood of the Jewish Church, —their altar of sacrifice,—their tabernacle and temple and their ceremonial observances will tell us. These embodied their religion ; and the heart and soul of that religion, the virtue and the value of it were, that they figured forth an atoning Saviour. Their various ordinances and yearly observances had for that people a central and a culminating point. There was a day in the Jewish calendar around which all other days, with their morning and evening sacrifices, revolved, as around the sun of their system. That day was the great day of Atonement. On that day and on no other for ages and for generations did the High Priest, and he alone, go into the most holy place, first of the Tabernacle and afterward of the Temple, disappearing from human sight within the veil. Standing there, as in the immediate presence of God, he made an atonement for the sins of the people with blood fresh from the altar. We need not trace the minuter features of our Jesus under all the symbols of a complicated ceremonial, though He was there, shadowing forth one function after another of His unchangeable office. It is enough for us to see Him in the Jewish High Priest on the day of the Atonement adumbrating from age to age the great fact that came to pass on earth when the fulness of the time was come. That was the figure of the Lamb slain from the foundation of the world, and that is the original and central conception of Jesus Christ.

I need not stop here to tell such a congregation as this how that conception was wrought out in the mission of Christ on earth. "When He came into the world He said 'a body hast Thou prepared me':" a body it was of flesh and blood, that our great High Priest need not enter the Holy Place without blood, but that with His own blood He might enter in once into heaven itself, having obtained eternal redemption for us. Such a conception necessitated a religion of ordinances. It must needs have had its temple and its altar and its priesthood to embody that conception,—to preserve it alive,—to transmit it from age to age, and to enable the world to recognize and to identify, when He came, "the Lamb of God that taketh away the sin of the world"—the Christ of the ages.

When in the fulness of time He came on the earth, turning figures into realities and prophecy into history, and embodying His religion in Himself, the daily sacrifice of a preparatory dispensation, the sacrificing priesthood, temple and altar, disappeared as shadows flee before the rising sun; so that when He left the earth He left behind Him the great central, wrought-out conception of His mission. He made provision for keeping it alive on the earth, that it should not vary, nor change, nor die out with the ages and the changes of time. To that end He left a Church on earth, with the record in it of His life and death. He bequeathed to that Church, and exalted into a visible, never ending memorial of Himself, the central conception of the Old Testament and the central truth of the New, namely, that His death was " a full, perfect and sufficient sacrifice, oblation and satisfaction, for the sins of the whole world." He gave commandment to His apostles that they should go and disciple all nations, baptizing them in His Name and teaching them to observe all things whatsoever He had commanded, of which things this Sacrament of the Altar was the chief. " Thus " to use the words of another,[1]—"sealing down upon them the impression of Christianity, stamping it down in sacraments and rituals and lessons and sermons, and leaving behind Him a visible example of the peace, the joy, the health that were to dwell in His household as the inheritance of His children."

What, I ask, in view of all this, was the religious upheaval that happened in the middle of the sixteenth century, great as it was, that any Christian man should be carried away by it to the point of believing that there is no power to determine what the faith of the

[1] Curteis Bampton Lectures, 1871.

churches or sects shall be? Has any age, or any people, or any Church, power to change the original conception of Christianity? Can it change the character or work of the Author of Christianity? Can it change the facts wrought out by Him on earth in pursuance of that everlasting conception of His religion? If so, then may churches, sects and individuals make their own creeds, and hold their own views. And to come further down, what is this century of ours, with all its boasted light and knowledge, that men should be moved and shaken out of this faith in Christ? What is its light of one hundred years, in comparison of the light of the ages of anticipation, and that of the ages of commemoration, centred and blended in the one Eternal Son of God,

"From out whose hand,
The centuries fall like grains of sand."

And now I go on to say that an embodied religion is the true religion for man. His twofold nature requires it, and God remembereth that we are dust. A memorial and a traditionary faith is the only one that may pass on from generation to generation, leaving its fruit behind it for the firmer anchoring of them that come after.

And here is the place to speak of those nineteenth century works and enterprises for human amelioration, and of that growing brotherhood of the race, of which so much is said in the interest of a sentimental religion. It is enough to say of human nature that it makes no leaps, and these are not our glory or those of our age. They are simply the crown of the Christian ages. The seed which has come to the fruit in our day was sown eighteen centuries ago. It started up in the little group of disciples gathered around the cross of Christ :—and it went on living and growing in the early Church. It was the spirit of sacrifice and gratitude in return for suffering and redeeming love. I know that love grew cold and faith waxed dim, and that ignorance and superstition crept over the Christianity of after times. It would have taken its everlasting flight from the earth, but that it was anchored and held fast by its creeds, its traditions and its ordinances. Out of this body of Christianity there rose up to illumine its darkest period, those piles of imperishable stone,—the Cathedrals of the Middle Ages. The body was preserved, and so the spirit survived, or revived, however misdirected and groping it may seem to this utilitarian age. The men who carved the cross of their redemption and wrought out the Creed of Christianity in monumental stone at a sacrifice of time and substance, that went on through generations, and with such indomitable pains and patience and perseverance, believed in an unchangeable kingdom of God on earth, and that the gates of hell should not prevail against it. They deemed Him worthy of their utmost honor and devotion, Who had redeemed them and their children unto God by His blood. The Cathedral rose, as it were, bodying forth afresh in something of its majesty, the Church of the living God. And there, with its outlines against the sky it stands to-day, to bind the earlier to the later ages of an unchanged religion. The same spirit, kindled at the same altar, and kept alive from generation to generation, has been and is still manifesting and embodying itself around that Church in the hospitals and the homes and the asylums that betoken the brotherhood of man in Jesus Christ.

In the face of all this, ignoring a historical religion with its Churches, its ordinances and its institutions, not a few of the men of science and the men of sentiment and the men of progress in these ends of the world, are curiously and skeptically taking up the Bible, as if that book were all that remained on earth to tell of Jesus Christ, and they know not what to make of Him. Let them all understand that the New Testament had a meaning given to it eighteen centuries ago, even before it was written, and that meaning has been working itself out in the lives of martyrs and confessors and saints from age to age down to this day. A long line of devout and holy men of whom the world was not worthy have lived, and not a few have sealed their testimony with their blood, and died in "the faith once delivered to the saints," and in the comfort of its reasonable, religious and holy hope. All these passed through the door of the one Baptism into the Church of Christ and all did eat the same spiritual meat, and drink the same spiritual drink from the same stricken Rock of Ages, which is Christ. Read your Bibles, indeed, and search the Scriptures, but search them whether these things are so. Read them understanding that that book was confided to the keeping and witness of a Church. Read the Bible in the light of history:—Read it in the light of the creeds and the traditionary signs and the never disused sacraments which have come to us along with it. And stop not there, but look back through your own family histories. Trace them through, perhaps, a long line of pious ancestry in this or in other lands, whose memory you hold in reverence, and who believed in Christ, walking in all His ordinances blameless, and know that you do not stand alone, with the Bible in your hands and the knowledge of to-day in your heads, but that you are bound with cords of gratitude and love to the Church of the living God, as to the Home on earth prepared for you before the world was. It is not the mere intellect of an inquirer in religion that needs the help I have endeavored to point out of a traditionary faith. His heart and his life, no less than his head, require it.

And now, I know that all I have put forward on this occasion is not demonstration either to the eye or the intellect. Remember then, I beseech you, as a final word, that in religion God does not take a man's intellect and deal with that only. The appeal of Him who made us and knows us, is to our souls and to all that is within us. And we are to receive all the testimony that comes to any and every faculty and susceptibility that He has given us. Surely, the combined testimony is overwhelming that this religion is from God, and has come down to this day as unchanged and unchangeable as Himself,—that it is, indeed, " The same Yesterday, To-day and Forever."

XVIII.

FAITH TRIUMPHING OVER DISAPPOINTMENTS.[1]

"These all died in faith not having received the promises, but having seen them afar off, and were persuaded of them and embraced them, and confessed that they were strangers on the earth."

"For they that say such things declare plainly that they seek a country."—Hebrews xi. 13, 14.

THESE, of whom the apostle speaks, were Abraham and his descendants Isaac and Jacob, the heirs with him of the same promise. And the promise was of the land of Canaan as an inheritance. "To thee and thy seed will I give it."

It must appear strange to the reader who takes these promises as they read, that these men did not receive that land nor possess it as an inheritance. The text declares, though the promise was made to them, that they failed of its realization.

It is said that they died in faith, but faith in what? In a proved and demonstrated impossibility? For they found themselves to the last

[1] See Robertson's Sermons, Vol. 1, p. 128. Boston, 1869.

but sojourners in a land that was not theirs. They had but a burying place in it, and that was purchased, not inherited. Touchingly is this faith described in the words, "not having received the promises, but having seen them afar off, they were persuaded of them and embraced them." That is, they held on to them and confessed at last that they were strangers and pilgrims not merely as respected the land of promise, but strangers and pilgrims on the earth. The writer adds, "For they that say such things declare plainly that they seek a country." Dying in the faith that the land of promise would be theirs, what country could they hope for at last but one beyond the grave? There is no other for the faith of a dying man. These men seemed to cling indeed through life to the shadow, as though the promise were tied to the land of Canaan. And so the chapter declares, that had they been mindful of the country, Chaldea, Egypt, from whence they came out, they might have returned, thus giving up at once and forever, the shadow they pursued. But they looked still forward for "Now," and that must mean as they neared their end, "they desire a better country, that is an heavenly."

I ask you, my brethren, in the light of this interesting account of the faith of the patriarchs, to trace to their upshot our own hopes of earthly good, to see how illusive and disappointing they are, and yet how they may help our faith in, and preparation for that better country, of which the writer of this epistle speaks. There is no doubt of the illusive ness of life's promises, and yet we are allowed by Almighty God to indulge a hope even to belief in them, and to act out that belief.

That life is illusive and disappointing, needs no proof to any one whose days have been long in the land. Much might be done to correct for the young and inexperienced, the unrealities and disappointments which they go on to encounter, if they would believe the testimony of age and experience. But they will not believe it. There is a tenacity of hope and faith and a vividness of imagination born with them in respect of their earthly future. Nothing can beat it out of them but an experience of their own, and even that often fails. And so the question comes up, is this illusion to be deplored? I think not, however sadly we who are older and wiser, find disappointment awaiting us. God is wiser than we are. He has given the young their instincts of earthly good. He has set that good before them as He set the land of Canaan before the patriarchs. And pursue it they will, undamped in their ardor and their eagerness, and unshaken in the belief that it will yet be theirs, by the disappointments that have come upon people before them. They go on undaunted in the pursuit of it, even by their own repeated failures.

So it will go on to be with our children, even as it has gone with us and our fathers. And the illusion will go on to the end of time. God has so made us. We have not saved ourselves, and we cannot save our children in this way from the pain and grief of loss and disappointment. And worse would it be for most of us, if we had thus been saved. For suppose, that by dint of the earnest endeavor of our fathers to undeceive us, with respect to the innocent gains and rewards of this life, we had been persuaded in early life to give up the hope, that perhaps we have now given up, that this life had any great prize for us. Suppose, that the efforts we have made for it had all been foreshewn to us to be vain, as very likely they have since proved to be. That would have put life before us in one important particular, as the truth has turned out to be, and stripped it of an illusion. Well, you incline to say, here then is one disappointment the less, and some pangs and griefs are spared us, with which we would have become acquainted. This is true. But where and what would we have been, is the question?

And I answer, just where any slave would be with all lively motive to his toil taken out of him—a drudge to the necessities of his lower nature—the higher and the nobler part of him unawakened and unprepared even to appreciate the immaterial and the spiritual that were in him. For let it be understood that very few of us can be drawn from the needful and drudging cares and occupations of a life that has no hope of a higher future in it, to fix our desires and affections upon a better. There is an intermediate object of pursuit between the grossness of earth and the invisibleness of heaven. No impossible bound from the one to the other is required of us. There is a stepping stone between them. And that is our hopes and expectations of worldly good. We may fail to reach that good. It may recede as we advance toward it. Its virtue does not consist in its being reached. For it may be reached as it often is, without affording one particle of the virtue hoped for in it. It may be grasped only to turn to dust and ashes in the hand. But striven for it will be with the instincts that God has given us, and which we cannot eradicate if we would, and I venture to say we ought not to eradicate if we could, for the lifting power that is in them.

We see in youth, life's promises afar off. We

are persuaded of them and we embrace them, be they of earthly gain, ambition or happiness in any of their thousand forms. They help us on our upward way. When heart and flesh fail, they keep us moving on till the time comes, when like the patriarchs, we have to confess that we are indeed pilgrims and strangers in a land that is not ours. So it is that the illusions of life have an educating power. It lies in the changes and chances of the world. In striving vainly for some good, our faith grows no less. It rather grows stronger with every successive disappointment, in the reality of something whose shadow has lured us on. Our immortality comes uppermost under such an experience. We gradually wake to a deathless longing for that which the world can never give, but which we believe God will yet give, if He did not make us in order to mock us to the last. And so, not having realized a single vivid promise of life; no Canaan, flowing with milk and honey having been given us to inherit, we nevertheless labor on toward it, it may be to the decline of life.

What will we do after such an experience of life as this? We cannot go back to the life we have lived. We would not live it again, if we could, any more than Abraham would have gone back to Ur of the Chaldees, or his descendants to the land of Egypt. No man cares to repeat a disappointing experience. Nothing therefore is left us, that is not utter despair, but to hold on to the promise of a good yet in the future, and die with our faith fixed upon it, and looking to see it realized in that better country to which we are bound. And so life's unrealities are exchanged at last for "the city that hath foundations, whose builder and maker is God."

Can we not say then of the illusions of life, that they are illusions, only in that they disappoint our hopes and wishes for certain or definite earthly good. We miss the good we seek, whether the objects we pursue are lost or gained. And this experience will keep us looking for some fresh field for the fulfilment of the promise.

We are like travelers approaching a turn in the road, or a wider prospect, to give us the view we seek, or bring us to the goal. Beyond that bend in the path, that clump of trees, that hill, the object of our long pursuit will present itself. From that point we shall begin to see the Canaan that we love, and taste at last its milk and honey. But the point is reached only for the blank to stretch itself away, and the goal to recede till it is within no reach but that of a determined faith. Such is life; life is an illusion and a dream. Blessed be God that it is not all illusion. Here, for example, is one whose faith long ago lifted him above his surroundings. The rewards to which he looked were the honors or emoluments of place; or the lodging of his name and fame in the affections of his kind. Well, years pass away and there at least stands the man. The hour has come to him, but without the honor or the gain. He stands there without one of life's coveted rewards. But is nothing gained? What will you say of the ideal early formed in that man's mind? What will you say of the power of sustained and concentrated faith? of the habits he has acquired of industry and perseverance? What will you say of the denial of his grosser self, and the sacrifice he has made of his ease and pleasure? What will you say of the character that must needs have been fashioned through years of hardness and self-denial, through perils and difficulties encountered and overcome? Small indeed are the honors or the rewards bestowed by other hands upon a man, in comparison of what, in the pursuit of them the man himself has grown to be. He has been spurning a life of ease and softness for one of hardness and lofty determination. He has gotten above the meannesses, the cowardice, and chicanery of men of lower motives; and who among you would exchange, what by the grace of God he is, for all the rewards he sought. At the core of such a life, be it outwardly one of illusion and disappointment from first to last, there is a worth and a value greater than all its lost rewards.

The Canaan he sought, that he misses. It is an illusion and a dream. But the solid and enduring land of promise thus gets within his reach. With faith still undying and stronger than death, he may all the more easily grasp the laurel and the diadem in the city which hath foundations. Not that the man of such a spirit and such an experience is sure to reach the eternal reality of the shadow he has been pursuing all his life. But such a spirit and such an experience are his best preparation for it. And his high hopes and expectations, and his higher instincts grown into a habit of aspiration, are such as must carry him, if he will only let them, above and beyond the rewards of earth. He is not far from the kingdom of heaven. That kingdom yields itself to earnestness, to perseverance, and to courage, and above all to a faith in the future such as this.

Take another instance of the disappointment which human life is and that at its best; that is to say, where the objects of hope and pursuit are gained, not lost. Take the not uncommon case of a man of business, gradually but surely gaining the fortune or position he set out to gain. He would be rich, not for the mere sake of riches, and so by degrees he is. He is able to retire to an establishment and an equipage, and to his pleasure grounds. He has found the Canaan he has loved so long. He is in the midst of it, he and his, all according to the picture of his fond imagination. And some years of earth are before him still, to enjoy his land of promise. But, were those few years of leisure and enjoyment all he has lived and labored for? Ah, my dear brethren, the milk and honey flowing freely round him, pall strangely on his taste. Is this all, he exclaims! The bitter answer is, that this is only the perishable husk of the land that has lain so long in his hope and his imagination. Take these things hence, he cries,—and give me some of the rest and peace I have longed and labored for. The man cannot go back. He must part with heart and hope, or go on still. And there is nowhere else to go, but to the reality of that which has been gradually gaining possession of him, and luring him on through the illusive and transitory to the solid and enduring.

A life like this lying behind him, with such a mockery round about him, surely ought to be enough to lead such a man to set his affections on things above. And it is enough. Such faith, in the future as his, has grown too strong to be smothered. It cannot die. Rather will it break through the veil of a mortal life. And blessed is the man who, not having received the promises, has been seeing them afar off all his life, and finds them at last "in the inheritance that is incorruptible, undefiled, and that fadeth not away."

The short and intelligible lesson of all this is to let the disappointments of life lead us early to anchor our faith and hope in the land that is very far off, so that we may be found declaring to all around us that verily we seek a country.

We may live lives of illusion and earthly disappointment here, but we shall have lived them "knowing in ourselves, that we have in heaven a better and an enduring substance."

XIX.

COMING TO JESUS BY NIGHT.

"The same came to Jesus by night."—St. John iii. 2.

FOLLOWING the words of the text is the account of a remarkable interview. I ask you to bear its particulars in mind, while I endeavor, with God's help, to gather from it some practical thoughts bearing on the attitude, as I believe, of not a few people everywhere, toward the Church of Christ.

This man came to Jesus by night, as the first mention made of him. The second mention presents him in the exercise of his office of a ruler of the Jews, at the Saviour's mockery of a trial. There his voice was heard in a feeble protest implying the same timidity or hesitation as his coming to Jesus by night.

His protest was so worded as to evade all responsibility whatever for the fate of one whom he had privately, and no doubt sincerely, acknowledged as a teacher sent from God. "Doth our law judge any man before it hear him and know what he doeth?" This is all he is recorded to have said to that bloodthirsty tribunal, and its effect was what might have been predicted. It simply provoked the sneer of his fellow rulers, "Art thou also a Galilean?"

The evangelist adds that "every man," Nicodemus of course included, "went to his own house." This was not the way to stand by a just and righteous man at a crucial point in his fate.

Once afterward Nicodemus appears on the scene. It was after the death and over the body of Jesus. He brought a mixture of myrrh and aloes to embalm His body. All else respecting Nicodemus is tradition—that he was baptized and became a Christian, lost his office and was banished from Jerusalem. It may be the truth, for there was working in him a sense of justice, a certain degree of candor, and no mere idle curiosity to know the truth, together with an appreciation of, and a respect for the character of Christ. But all this with an underlying hesitation of mind, and a fear of man which kept him from taking a bold and open step in the line of his better nature, till some one else should break the way, or till all fear of personal harm or inconvenience was removed. This happened after Christ's death and on the occasion of His burial, when Nicodemus was ready to act out the good that was in him.

Such then was the character with which our Saviour had to deal in this nocturnal interview; and while we must assume that he laid down in what he said, a fundamental principle of His religion of universal application, we may believe that He here propounded it in terms the best suited to the needs of the man before Him —that He laid His hand on the weak spot in the character of Nicodemus, when He told him that a man must be born again, and born of water and of the spirit, in order to enter the Kingdom of God. He referred here to the inward change required by His religion, but also to the outward and changed relations to the world to which a man must also conform, in order to be a follower of His. For a new birth, a birth in which water was to play its part, whatever the inward change, certainly implies changed external relations. And this latter change was more than Nicodemus had counted on. It was more than he was ready for. He was bidden to take a step here entirely at war with the caution and secrecy that marked his visit to the Saviour. Whatever else discipleship involved, he found from this interview, that for him it involved an open confession of Christ, and a change unpleasantly affecting his earthly interests, or his social position and surroundings, and in order to take the stand required, he must rid himself, at one blow, of all fear of earthly consequences. His, "How can these things be?" may be interpreted as also questioning why they must be. And here it is that Nicodemus has many a follower to-day. He, a ruler, ought at least to have known how one of another faith and nation was received as a proselyte of the Jewish religion. For Baptism was one of those earthly things that a master of Israel should have understood, and how it severed a man from his old surroundings on earth and changed his religious posture in the face of the world. But so it happened, that here on the threshold of the heavenly kingdom Nicodemus stumbled and fell, and so he failed to lay hold of the first truth to be acted out in Christ's religion.

Now the sacrament of Baptism may stand for all the signs and badges of Christian discipleship of which it is the head and the beginning. And I would hold these up to you who are before me, not only as tokens to the outside world, of fealty to Christ, but tests of the sincerity of the subjects of them—as something by which all of us may know what manner of spirit we are of.

I will begin by saying that I believe there is a great deal of sincere regard for, and belief in the religion of Christ and in His virtue as a Saviour, by people—by grown up and growing up men especially, who nevertheless do not let the world know it, and are careful not to let it be known in any open way whatever. To a casual observer, they seem to receive the Scriptures as though in them they have eternal life, and they hear the Gospel preached as though there were virtue in it. They, no doubt, wonder at times how these things can be, as though all were a mystery; and at other times as though awake to the possibility that they may indeed be so. They would fain have their lives brightened by the hope in Christ, and they cherish this hope, especially in loss, affliction and death, as all they can resort to by way of consolation. And yet they are not ready to make this hope a sure one at any real cost, a cost to their inclinations, or convenience, the cost of giving up any of their plans, associations or habits of life. And so they live on, and nobody is the wiser as to what they think or believe or mean to do, or how much or how little they care for any of these things. And they do not mean that others shall know. They keep their thoughts and such intentions as they have to themselves, till they come to die. And then for the first time we learn of a vast many, that they have thought more seriously and deeply on the subject of religion, than was ever known to their most intimate friends. On beds of death they often give their first utterance to the secret of a lifetime. Their regret is then first made known, that they have never taken the open step that Christianity requires. That the regret is poignant there is no room to doubt, however its poignancy may be veiled under a show of calmness and resignation. They appear to die in hope and try to die with as much hope as they can to their own comfort, also to that of the friends they leave behind them. Baptized they may have been or may not, and if in unconscious infancy with the vows of Baptism forgotten and its privileges ignored through life, neither the fact nor its remembrance can much help them in the hour of death. I would, if possible, convince them how little worth in death this sort of faith is, and what a poor trembling hope must come out of it for a happy hereafter.

I would be glad to believe that very few coming to Church from week to week, have no better faith or surer hope than this. But I fear they are many. They may perhaps see a likeness to themselves in what has been said, and possibly no one else can even guess the spiritual posture they occupy to-day. Some of their friends may live long enough to know what the secret of their lives has been. Weighty words may yet be heard from their lips, and unexpected words, if words do not fail them in their last hour. Words of comfort and words of hope they may be, but words they must be out of timid and trembling hearts, when they ought to be such as will let them go the way of all the earth, in sure and certain hope of their resurrection to eternal life, through Jesus Christ our Lord.

And so it happens that we see many coming to the house of God, and going away as though caring for no further step beyond this in the face of the world. But many do and must care. They care like Nicodemus. Some care even like the woman in the crowd, who would fain have taken away her blessing by stealth, and who felt within herself that she was blest, but who found at last that she had yet an open confession to make, and was not permitted to go healed without it. No, they have been only coming to Jesus by night, as the most and the best that they have done. They have done it indeed often. They may even do it habitually. But as often as they come, they are met by the words, " Verily, verily, I say unto you, except a man be born anew of water and of the Spirit, he cannot enter into the kingdom of God," and that means, except you come out to the light of day, with an open transfer of your faith and trust and with no fear or shame before your eyes, how indeed can you enter the kingdom of God?

It is indeed a kingdom not of this world. But it is a kingdom in it, and has its signs, few and feeble it may be, to the eye of sense. And the fewer and feebler they are to human sight, so much the more need that they be brought out and held up continually in the light of day, lest the reality be lost altogether out of the world, and not a trace be left of the existence on earth of either a kingdom of heaven or its Divine Founder.

But I set out to shew further, that this open committal to the religion of Christ is a test by which to try oneself and to know what manner of spirit he is of. As such no doubt it was propounded to Nicodemus by the Author of that religion in person. He came to Jesus by night, and had he been encouraged to come again by the promise of a nearer and a closer acquaintance with one whom he acknowledged to have come from God, this seeker for truth would no doubt have done so gladly, and enjoyed the secret and the sacred intercourse. But, He who was thus sought unto could not thus be reached for the truth, and hope, and salvation that were in Him.

And he who came to test and try the Saviour of the world, to his secret satisfaction, found himself tried and tested at his first and faintest approach, in a way that searched his soul.

Will you indeed be my disciple? Then come to me openly, and change your allegiance. Let it be known to what kingdom you belong. Waver not between your fear of man and your love for the truth. He who confesseth me, he it is that honoreth me, and not he who comes to me by night, or comes to me by stealth, that he may serve himself with what he may find in me, and go his way, hoping to be healed of what sin or infirmity he has.

This then is the easiest and the surest test by which many of you may try yourselves. It may not be to all of you a test of your sincerity. Nicodemus, who failed under it, was yet sincere. It may not serve to show whether you have the fear of man before your eyes, for the Christian confession is no losing or disreputable thing at this day, that any man or woman should hesitate to make it on that account. But it is a test of your love to Christ, and of a true regard for Him. "If ye love me, keep my commandments." And it is a test of faith. You must believe in things that you have no ability to reason out, and simply trust in the word of Him who ordained them. This is the test of a mind made up to be a Christian, and here perhaps above all, a sure test is wanted.

For many of you want to be Christians. Some think they are such perhaps, because they are baptized members of the Church. But this hovering for years along the border ground, between the Church and the world, is simply ignoring your Christian character. It cannot be explained, save on the supposition of minds not yet made up. Dost thou renounce? Dost thou believe? And wilt thou obey? Upon these questions the made up mind or the will is wanting. There is with you, if not the fear of man, then a fear of yourselves, or a doubt which dishonors Christ, because it doubts the truth of His promise; "As thy day so shall thy strength be." And so, dreading the effect of the daylight upon your not yet made up minds, you feel your way along the borders of the night, thankful if you may for a while longer escape observation and evade something, be it more or less of solemn responsibility.

And now I ask you who have perhaps been going in and out of the house of God for years, without coming any nearer to the test laid down for you by your Lord and Saviour, what do you think upon serious reflection of a state of mind like this?

Look at it once more in the man whose character we have glanced at on this occasion. He knew, he said, as you also believe, that no man could do those miracles except God were with him. And yet knowing this, he came to Jesus by night, because he was afraid or ashamed to be seen coming. With similar feelings, and yet with the same conviction and belief he ventured inoffensively to ask the bloodthirsty men around him, whether their law judged a man before it heard him, and knew what he did.

Whereupon, under a sneer from his fellows, he disappeared and left an innocent man to his death. This was the upshot of a wavering mind. One last thing Nicodemus did because he could do it safely and go his way. He was ready to show respect to the memory of a good man, who no longer needed it, by his hundred pounds' weight of spices and aloes.

The voice of Him who was thus treated while living and after He was dead, would seem to come sounding in the ears of Nicodemus, and all who are like him "If any man will come after me, let him deny himself, and take up his cross daily, and follow me."

There are many among us who seem to wish to show their love for Christ, if at no other time, on the occasion devoted to His birth and resurrection, with their sentimental tributes to His memory, which mean nothing to themselves, and less than nothing to Him. Understand, once for all, that we are not Christ's disciples because of our feelings toward Him, our observance of social or religious proprieties, our respectful manners, or our ceremonial decency. All this is consistent with entire non-committalism to His cause.

I close beseeching all such to break out of the secrecy and the constraint of coming to Jesus by night, and no longer to go on suffering the self-reproach and humiliation intolerable to self-respecting men and women. Have done, once for all, with such a posture, and say openly what was betokened for many of you on your unconscious heads, that you are not ashamed to confess the faith of Christ crucified, and that you are ready henceforth to fight manfully under His banner, and to continue His faithful soldiers and servants to your life's end.

XX.

THE CONVERSION OF ZACCHEUS OR THE POWER OF SYMPATHY.

"And when Jesus came to the place, He looked up and saw him, and said unto him, Zaccheus make haste and come down: for to-day I must abide at thy house. And he made haste and came down and received Him joyfully."—St. Luke xix. 5, 6.

THE New Testament nowhere records the case of a speedier and at the same time a completer change in a human being than this that took place in Zaccheus. We know what sort of man he had been, from his sudden resolution to be merciful to the poor, and to restore fourfold the proceeds of his injustice. He resolved on the spot to disburden himself of riches gained at the expense of his conscience. The Jewish people had a firm conviction that the Roman government had no right to levy upon them any tax at all. Zaccheus was a recreant Jew to accept the office. Having accepted it, however, he made the most of it, as a man will who compromises his character and his position for the sake of money. He regards himself as having no character to lose, and the only compensation for loss of character being a money gain, he is no longer careful of the way he gains it. He will thus pay himself for his loss of caste, and there is a revengeful pleasure in taking out of the pockets of those who hate and despise him the means of payment. He will let them understand if they will no longer tolerate him, that they must pay the cost of his social ostracism. That Zaccheus felt the sting of this we cannot doubt, and as he grew richer he felt it the more keenly, because he saw that riches were not gaining, but rather losing him social advantages.

Men who have no standing but that of money, are commonly ready to pay for social consideration. They feel the lack of it the more, because they have money; and a judicious use of money will go far toward giving them what they want. In the estimation of his community Zaccheus had got too low down for his money to do this, or else money failed at that day of the virtue it has with us. Here then he was, his money failing to give him consequence, and among a crowd of people where his smallness of stature appeared at its greatest disadvantage. Add to this the odium attached to his occupation, and we behold him a target for the jeers and reproaches of those who knew him. Possibly his curiosity had gotten the better of all other feelings for the moment, or it might have been an impulse such as more than once occurred in that August Presence, and which he could not account for, that determined him to see Jesus,—who He was. At any rate here he was with the pressure hot and heavy upon him of his ill repute,—a rich and recreant Jew,—an oppressive and a dishonest man,—a notorious and hated character, compelled to read in the faces of the crowd their estimate of himself, and feeling it to the core of a bitter heart.

Now, the astonishing thing to us in the conversion of Zaccheus, when we think a moment, is not that he came down joyfully from the sycamore tree at the bidding of Christ, or that he came at the same moment out of the miserable and mercenary bonds that had bound him up in himself. Because we can well imagine the suffering of such a condition as his had been, the isolation, the disgrace, the chafing and the bitterness, and that he had possibly been longing for something that would reinstate him in the good opinion of his neighbors, restore to him his self-respect and help him to discharge his conscience of a heavy burden. It is very accountable that he should have behaved himself as he did under the circumstances of the call made upon him.

The remarkable thing is that he was singled out on that occasion by our Lord for the notice he received. It was as unexpected as anything could possibly be to him:—It was equally unexpected to the crowd around him. It was a wonderful stroke,—a surprising specimen of "a word in season." After the open offer of Christ to be his guest, all is natural and all is accountable.

And after all, my brethren, what was the word that opened this sealed and selfish heart, and wrought the conversion of a sinner from the error of his ways? It was but a word of human sympathy that any man might have spoken with effect who knew the heart of Zaccheus, and therein it had its only advantage over such words of ours. In nothing else did that word differ from ours, any more than our sympathy differs from that of Christ, and it differs only in degree. It was the human in Zaccheus that was touched by the human that was in Christ. Its power lay in the fact that being a man and touched with the feeling of our infirmities, Christ was able thus to succor and to save a fellow man.

And so I want, my brethren, to present our Saviour here as an example of the power of sympathy. It has been truly said that we really do very little to help one another in this world. Our time is mostly taken up with our own things. But there is something of little cost and of more worth than a sacrifice of time and substance for our fellow men. In the case of Zaccheus a passing word was all the cost that appeared, but it lifted that man out of his sufferings and out of his sins. It filled his heart with gratitude and restored him to himself. It brought him once more within the pale of human society and sympathy from a state of ostracism and alienation. It filled a dry and shriveled heart with hope and happiness.

Let me go a little further with an explanation of the sudden and happy change wrought upon Zaccheus by the sympathy of Christ. Its power will be the easier understood if we consider the import of the address that was made to him,—"Make haste and come down, for to-day I must abide at thy house." It was not the mere attention and notice of our Lord that touched him so deeply, though that must have been as grateful as it was unexpected. It was the offer made to him in the most touching of all possible ways of a friendly acquaintance. It was the offer in the presence of that indifferent and contemptuous crowd to be his guest. Zaccheus saw in Christ a man of repute, if he saw nothing more; and it was such a man that had singled him out for a courteous notice,—

and more, here was a reputable man who publicly declared his willingness to be under social obligations to him. The friendly greeting alone was enough to open a selfish and a thristy heart. But the bidding that followed went to the depths of that heart. It sent conviction to the bottom of it, that here was a word of kindness to the sinner that came from the heart and meant something more than common civility. There could be no affectation about such an offer as this. The offer was made in the face of the world, to meet a friendless and hated man on a level of mutual courtesy and respect. Nothing could go further toward proving the sincerity of such an offer than that this stranger was to be the guest, and he, the publican and sinner, his host.

There is yet another touch of nature here too important to be passed over, and which the incident as narrated discloses:—"Forasmuch as he also is a son of Abraham." Refraining from all allusion to the fact of his odious office and his extortionate conduct, our Lord brought out to view the underlying truth of the common ancestry of Zaccheus with Himself. This put them fairly on a social level, and entitled Zaccheus to the courtesy which was shown him. It put the publican at his ease in the presence of One who claimed with himself, to be a son of Abraham.

Here then, my dear brethren, stands our example of the proper treatment of our fellow men, if we would make them better men. No doubt, much can be done for the amelioration of our race by the working around and upon them of the standing ordinances of the gospel. I have no wish to undervalue any of them, certainly not that of preaching the gospel to the poor and the sinful, and we may learn here that that preaching is the most effectual which deals with men as though they had hearts of flesh and blood as the most accessible thing about them. This ordinance of the gospel, which requires the living man to come in personal contact with the minds to be influenced, has its best account in the power of sympathy. The sincere and cordial word which comes fresh from the heart through living lips, and reaches the heart, assuring the hearer that he and the preacher are kin, carries with it a power to arrest the attention, which no written words can have, not even, and I speak it with reverence, the Scripture itself. What is first wanted is not written assurances, however convincing or full in their appreciation of human needs:— but it is spontaneous assurances, finding vent for themselves and sounding out through living lips, and thus doing something on the instant for both speaker and hearer. This is what opens men's hearts and moves them, while the other, at most, only convinces. And the movement is owing to the power of sympathy. The heart thus touched will respond, though the intellect is yet to be reached. And that response is active when the reason and judgment, however convinced of the truth, may never carry the man over to the doing of that truth. And so it is that it has pleased God through the foolishness of preaching to save them that believe. They want more than mere belief which the Written Word affords, they want motive to act at once, and mere truth will not help them here. But sympathy will. Selfishness must be started out of itself, and no selfishness was ever thus moved but by a contact in some living way with the "Charity that seeketh not her own." If this be true then every Christian can be a most effectual preacher of the gospel. And he is bound to be. I do not mean that he is to set out, as, though it were his mission, upon the work of saving the lost,—that assumption on his part will defeat the end. He will be regarded as acting in the line of his profession, or merely in the way of duty, and he will find more hearts closed than open to him. The heart of man is a very sensitive thing,—no assumed or implied superiority will cause that heart to open, however pure the intention. It will close up against such an advance upon it. Nor will it do to make acquaintance with the lawless and disreputable for the avowed purpose of taking them to task for the character they bear, or for the things of which they are guilty. They know what they are, and if they know what we are, we can address them as though they were worthy of our courteous notice. Indeed, there is no other way to find them open to the sympathy that is in us; and that ought to be, like that of our Master, ever ready to go out from us. The disciple will be here as his Master, who regarded men not so much as sinners, guilty and to blame, as creatures lost and to be found. He found Zaccheus to the bottom of his soul, by going behind his character and behind his sins and by regarding him as simply lost,—lost to society and lost to self-respect. He looked upon the publican as a suffering rather than a sinning man. This it was that roused a Saviour's sympathy, and it must rouse ours if we would have it a power for good. Our first word will then be, whatever our second,—"a word in season," if it be no more than a mere greeting of civility. It may not be so much as a word:—a gesture of attention, a courteous motion, will sometimes open a human heart. And our respectful hearing of a tale of woe, or of a series of troubles and vexations that flow out of a full heart, or a confession of sin and of wrong, are often a relief for which the patient listener will receive the thanks of many a hardened man and woman. There is a mystery about this result of which you can only say Such is the power of sympathy. The attentive listener to a story will be surprised to find that he has made by his silence during the recital, a grateful friend. If it is a case of poverty, that poverty, I know, may be relieved by money. But the heart is not thus relieved, nor can the hearts of the poor be changed or opened by mere money benefactions. This experiment is tried often. It is tried almost everywhere in times of privation and among whole classes of our fellow men. Scant thanks come out of it, and no softened feeling. The contrary is oftener the truth. The almoner of a charitable society, or a wealthy man or woman may go through the poverty-stricken districts of a city and scatter, as they fondly think, blessings in their path. And the blessings they dispense, while grasped with eagerness, have been known to turn into curses behind their backs. There is, of course, relief to hunger and nakedness, but there is the same pent-up and smouldering fire in the heart, of envy and anger and rebellious discontent. The animal is relieved, while the man fails to be touched. Here is the root of the conflict of poverty with property, and of labor with capital. The angels of peace in this world are they who go with open hearts and it may be with slender purses through those same streets, listening respectfully and silently to the tales of woe, the stories of poverty and misfortune, of sickness and death, of sin and crime and disgrace which they have to tell. In the one case we have, or we may have, all that time and money can do, without one cordial response;— in the other we may have nothing but a single touch of human feeling. But it is a touch that reaches, and by the grace of God it may prove a touch that saves the lost. It is a touch that makes the whole world kin.

As members of the Christian household, we hear the most persistent demands, and when we do not hear them, we know very well the craving that exists for more of society and more of sympathy. A cultivation of the social element is demanded by and among Christian people. People want to know their neighbors and their brethren. But more than this they want to be known and noticed by their neighbors and their brethren. Those who have their own social circle of sympathetic friends feel this need less cravingly than others, and they may have no sufficient appreciation of the feelings that exist around them. And therefore, they do not put themselves out of the way or turn aside in order to minister to it. It is looked upon as mere ceremony that is demanded, with nothing valuable and least of all nothing that is Christ-like in it.

But what is the social element? What is this knowing of our neighbors and our brethren and what is the being known by them and the noticing of them, the want of which is sometimes bitterly felt? It is but the exhibition and working out of Christian sympathy, —the sympathy of Christ Himself. It is using the power that is in every one of us, by virtue of our humanity, for doing good. It is putting in motion the most powerful agency of our holy religion toward the amelioration of our fellow men. It is using the weapon that, in the case of Zaccheus, found its way to the bottom of the heart of selfishness and malignity and turned it into a well-spring of gratitude and kindly charity.

One additional word: The example of Christ here, as elsewhere, is an example of perfection. He went to the extreme of becoming the guest of this poor, sinful man, in order to let him receive in full tide the constraining power of His human sympathy. But He did it also to let us know the way we are to reach men's hearts. "We are members one of another" and there are times when this membership must shew itself like His, who is the Head of the Body, in all its glory and in all its beauty. "Pure religion and undefiled before God and the Father is this, to visit the fatherless and widows in their affliction and to keep himself unspotted from the world." This in its literalness cannot be done, and it need not be done by every follower of Christ, but the cup of cold water for thirsty souls, that he has put into our hands by virtue of our common humanity, is bound to be forthcoming in every trial and in every need that overtakes a neighbor. This little thing is a mighty power for good. There belongs to it the promise of a heavenly reward. "Is any afflicted among you? Is any sick? Is any poor? And especially if any do err from the truth, and one convert him, let him know, that he who converteth the sinner from the error of his ways, shall save a soul from death and hide a multitude of sins."

XXI.

SERMON FOR ALL SAINTS' DAY.

"I would not have you ignorant brethren, concerning them that are asleep."—1 Thess. iv. 13.

AMONG the signs of this ignorance or of our little faith, is the way we let ourselves think and feel concerning them that are asleep. For awhile we feel our loss and think often of our friends departed: but it is too often as of friends who once lived and are dead to live no more. The veil which hides them from our sight grows darker and denser and the light which comes through it dimmer and colder, till it fades into a mere recollection of their forms and faces. Any hope that we shall meet them again is a vague and flickering hope. Some of us try to set ourselves against this tendency to forgetfulness, with a feeling of its selfishness, coldness and ingratitude. Others willingly let dumb forgetfulness creep over them, lest their remembrance turn into unhappiness;—and still others let their dead go out of mind at once, as though their death were annihilation.

I need hardly say that there is little preciousness in a hope or remembrance like this. And the indifference we sometimes discover is simply shocking, not to the Christian believer only, but to every sensitive human being. Better a heart that aches than one past feeling. Better a morbid hankering over friends departed. Better the sad solace of picturing them day by day as they were in form and feature and character,—till our eyes grow dim with tears, and our hearts grow faint with longing for a return of that which can never be.

But better than all is the solace afforded us in the Church of God, by the truth she teaches and brings continually before her sorrowing children, concerning them that are asleep. For it is as true of the departed that they live now, as that they were once alive; or that they shall live again. They live though they die,—that is the true solace. They are asleep to us only as we think of them in the body. They are not asleep to themselves nor to God. And they would not be asleep to us one sad or solitary moment, were it not that we ignore the truth, or because of our little faith. For we are ignorant concerning them that are asleep, if we think of them only that they were, or that they will be hereafter, when the earth and the sea shall give up their dead. They are living now. This is the life brought to light in the gospel, and of which the apostle would not have us ignorant.

Blessed are the dead who died in the Lord! Not because they are dead knowing nothing and feeling nothing,—not because pain or decay has done its work upon a body which can suffer no more, but because they have passed the waves of this troublesome world and are at rest,—and blessed too because their works do follow them. The good they did here and the examples they set here are yielding fruits which come home to them one by one, where they are, to their ever increasing comfort and their joy. And so, instead of living here where—

"Man never is but always to be blest,"

they are living there, blest ever more and more of God.

We are members of a Church whose creed and formularies emphasize this comforting truth respecting the holy departed. Whatever has become of the truth elsewhere, the distinctive doctrine of an intermediate state has ever been put prominently forward in the historical body of Christ. The time was when she was wont in her services to read aloud the names of the departed, calling a roll, as though of living men and women sitting at the Lord's table partaking still, only out of sight, of the one bread and one cup of the one Communion. Every liturgy of early Christianity that has come down to us, provides for special mention of the departed, with prayers for their repose in peace, and for heavenly light to shine upon them. We have not the prayers in our Communion office, nor place there for the names of the departed, —nor is it proposed to put them there. This portion of the service was dropped at the time of the Reformation, as being liable to abuse as it had been abused, to a doctrine of purgatory, to masses for the dead and other superstitious usages.

But we have retained one distinct and precious reminder of the saints departed, and it finds a response in every loving heart when "we bless God's holy name for all his servants departed this life in His faith and fear," and pray, not perhaps, so much for them as for ourselves, when we ask for "grace so to follow their good examples that with them we may be partakers of His heavenly Kingdom." But more than this. We have retained in our Calendar a day sacred to the remembrance of the departed. Its observance is spreading in these days among us. It is a standing protest against the Sadduceeism of the age in which we live. It helps to a healthy reaction from it. It declares that no hopeless, materialistic thought of the dead shall enter here,—nor can it disturb the faith of the people of God in the precious truth that we live though we die.

There are Christian bodies in which the intermediate state receives scant notice, as though the sleep of death were too profound to know any awakening but the trumpet call to judgment;—as though either ignorance or indifference prevailed even here, concerning them that are asleep. What will they do with the struggle and the cry of nature here for light in a dark place?—and with the blind gropings of spiritualism in which the dead must be galvanized into life and kept living through jugglery? For spiritualism on its better side is a demand for the truth which this Church of ours has in store to give to those bereft of friends and who are breaking their hearts and depriving themselves of all hope and comfort, and not seldom giving up the very religion of Jesus Christ as presented to them.

There is a cure for all this,—and it is to lay hold of the truth as to the state and condition of departed saints. That truth is, that they are still living parts of the body of Christ, which is His Church, alive and in His keeping all the days of their appointed time until their last change come. And it is a change for which they are represented in Scripture as looking and waiting in the intermediate state, to wit:—the consummation of their bliss in body and soul in Christ's everlasting Kingdom.

And now let us inquire briefly into that necessarily obscure and, never on earth to be fully understood, article of our faith, the Communion of Saints.

First, who are the saints? They are not then, faultless men and women only, as we know them here. Neither are they the soft, shrinking and effeminate among men and women of whom we sometimes say and oftener feel that they are too shrinking to battle with the world they live in;—that it is too harsh and unfriendly a world for them, and, therefore, blessed are they for they go to a better. But they are such men and women as are named in that chapter of the Hebrews which we read this morning. Among them are Abraham, Noah, Jacob, Moses, the harlot Rahab, Gideon, Barak, Samson, Jephtha, David. That shows us of what sort are the saints. They were sinners. Some of them sinned grievously, and all were compassed with their respective infirmities of the flesh. The one good thing that marked all of them alike, was that they had the will to struggle with those infirmities;—they had faith to believe in the power and promise of God to make that

SERMON FOR ALL SAINTS' DAY. 243

struggle a final success. And they had patience and endurance as seeing Him who is invisible. They suffered, some of them openly and others obscurely, but all were examples of how much could be borne and done in this world in the faith of some better thing to come. Out of weakness this made them strong; and the crown of every character was this, that they had no fall from which they did not rise again. This made them saints. And it makes them still. When we look round about us and see such people to-day,—no better we think than we are, or might easily be if we had a mind, it may seem strange to call them saints.

But we feel that death passing over characters like these purifies and sublimates them; and then we forget the sins and defects of character which beset them here. It is a right feeling,—for their faults and defects were part of the burden of the flesh, of which each one knew and felt the weight for himself, and fought against it, but from which all are now and forever free. So that there the character shines forth for what it is. It has got away from its earthly cleavings and cast aside its earthly mould, even as the sun rises and clears itself from the clouds and mists that hang round the horizon. And so it is equally a natural and a right feeling that glows in loving bosoms toward good men and women, especially of our own kith and kin and of our households departed. We know what they were at bottom, under all they appeared to men to be, and we number them instinctively among God's elect. Such as these, and guileless children are the saints for whom we bless God's holy name that they live though they die, and that they have entered into a land of rest.

And what in the second place is our communion with them? Here I would tread cautiously, as in a dark place, and leave much untouched that we know not now but shall know hereafter:—one thing I may say and that is, that our communion consists partly in this, that an inspiration, as from the lives of our departed friends comes into our own. It is not the strong motive to right living that comes out of the redeeming life and death of Christ our Saviour. It is lower than that. Nevertheless, it stands next to it;—for next to redeeming love is the power of fraternal sympathy. Such is the power over us of good men and women while in the flesh. It reaches its height when we are drawn toward them departed, in love and gratitude. The hero, it is said, commands our admiration and the teacher challenges our reverence; but the saint awakens our sympathy. We cannot feel, perhaps, with the other characters. We may lack the gifts of the one and the knowledge and wisdom of the other, and so we stand outside the peculiar experiences that belong to them. But we can have communion and fellowship with every frail human struggler after goodness, to our heart's core. We know him for what he often is,—"destitute, afflicted, tormented, persecuted, but not forsaken; cast down, but not destroyed." This experience we may know to the bottom. And nothing is in the way of the coming to us in full and unchecked tide, the inspiration of the lives of good men and women that have ended,—and not those only that have ended. "Be ye steadfast in the faith," writes an apostle,—"knowing that the same afflictions are accomplished in your brethren that are in the world." We are bidden here not merely to look to those who have gone before us, but to brethren struggling at our side, for the help we need to stand our ground.

What an animating scene is brought before us, partly visible to the eye of sense, and all spread out plainly to the eye of faith, in "The Communion of Saints"? In addition to the life going on within the veil, comes before us the field of battle on earth, and the faithful strugglers here toward the rest that remaineth for the people of God. And so we are compassed about with a great cloud of witnesses. All around us, to the eye of faith, is life and there is no death.

> "One army of the living God
> To His command we bow,
> Part of His host have crossed the flood
> And part are crossing now."

Let me say that what we lack of the power of sympathy from our brethren that are in the world, is supplied by the added influence that comes from them after their deaths. While they live, they are so entirely of us that the inspiration of their lives lacks the religious element of reverence, and we need that. Familiarity with living men and women, however good they may be, breeds something of indifference, sometimes of irritation toward their peculiarities of temper or character, not to speak of their open faults and derelictions. We know indeed, the good that is in them, and can do justice to their motives and characters, and yet it requires the mysterious change wrought by death, to clear away obstructions to the full force of their good examples. When the unseen hand of God has taken and translated them, then awe and reverence tinge our feelings toward them; and then it is that the inspiration of their lives comes into ours with power. We see how this works in the minds of children. They need no reminder for a while of the will and mind of a departed father or mother. They walk softly, reverently and circumspectly in the path of filial duty marked out to them. Reproof from parents living pass by them as the idle wind. After the last dread change, it comes clothed with new and quickening power over sons and daughters. And this added power lays hold of children of a larger growth. Reckless sons and careless daughters whom living parents scarcely had power to control, feel the power at last. It comes to them out of the land where sin and earthliness are done away. It is the more powerful, because coming from hearts and lips closed in death. And so it has happened, and it will go on to be true, that from the careless and disobedient, and from sons and daughters hitherto reckless of things unseen, will falter forth over a grave, or over the thought of parents sleeping in the dust, the prayer of All Saints—" O God grant us grace to follow them in all virtuous and godly living."

A final word of exhortation from what has now been said. The one lack we have in this world in order to wean us from it and win us to a better, is faith in the invisible. By faith it was that the men and women in that grand chapter of the saints became what they were and what they are. They endured as seeing Him who is invisible. Without faith, whatever else we have, we are girt about on earth only with the enemies of our souls, and the opposers of our progress. We are like Elisha's servant surrounded by the chariots and horses of the enemy. And like him, we are fain to cry out —" Alas, Master, what shall we do?"

In answer to this cry, He will open our eyes, and we shall behold the mountain full of horses and chariots of fire round about us. His words will sound in our ears—" Fear not! for they that be with us are more than they that be with them." O Lord, open thou our eyes that they may rest upon Thine own, the central Figure in the mount of God, and upon that cloud of witnesses—

> "Whose crowns of living glory
> Are lit with rays from Thee."

www.ingramcontent.com/pod-product-compliance
Lightning Source LLC
Chambersburg PA
CBHW070247230426
43664CB00014B/2430